The Ralls County Line:

sketches from a rural mid-American Odyssey

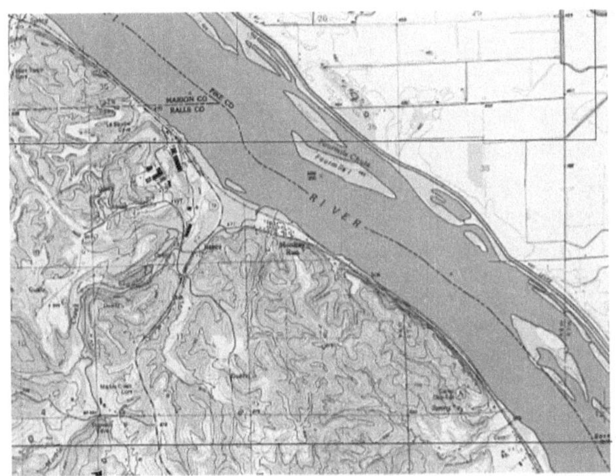

by Jude MacAllen Tatman

Spartan Press

Spartan Press

Kansas City, Missouri

spartanpress.com

Acknowledgments:

A few of these poems have appeared in some ideation or the other in the following publications, to which the poet thanks with a grateful nod—

Periodicals:

Envy's Sting, Green Tower Press, 1986.

WILDSound Writing Festival, *Body Image Poetry Contest 2025.*

Chapbook:

Echoes- selected poems & short stories 1984-2023, a Wylde Irish Project, 2025.

Anthology:

A Drop of the Pure; Gumbo Bottoms Single Pot Still Society presents. Jon Freeland and Jason Ryberg, editors. OAC Press & Spartan Press KC, 2025.

There are numerous folks, kith and kin who have helped me on this journey out of rural Missoura and back, some are gone, some have traveled on, some are still with me in one way or the other.

Greatest appreciation to the Program Director and Assistant Program Director, University of Nebraska Creative Writers' Workshop MFA Program, Kevin Clouther and Diane Holliday. Kevin, for giving me a chance, as well as sage guidance as I familiarized myself with the world of creative writing, and Diane, for helping this 20th Century wanderer navigate the 21st Century's Information Technologies: both have been wonderful and valued teachers, as well as friends, during and continuing after my studies at UNO.

Dr. William "Bill" Trowbridge, my first mentor at UNO, as well as my first creative writing professor as an undergrad at Northwest Missouri State University. It was "Doc," as I have known him for forty years, who recommended me for acceptance to UNO's Writer's Workshop. His help in "relearning" the art, history, and role of the English language in the sculpting words into emotions was then and now most appreciated. I am honored to have him as a mentor and friend.

Every sailing ship needs an anchor, and for my journey towards my MFA, Dr. Graham Faust was that anchor. My third semester mentor at UNO, I am indebted to him for his stalwart advice in how to tighten up my writing, teaching self-examination, discipline, and critique of my own work –something that was sorely lacking in my early attempts at the craft. His presence at the Workshop was most rewarding. I have one regret; I wasn't able to spend more time in his company during my final residency.

If Graham was my anchor, then my second and forth semester mentor let me hoist the sails and explore; Professor Elizabeth A. I. Powell was my most influential mentor with the Workshop. Liz allowed me to further investigate my own being, pushing me to be emotionally honest in my writing. Her role as my thesis advisor was instrumental in forming my manuscript for this collection. Liz taught me how to be my own person as a writer and poet, and to have patience – especially with myself. I will be ever grateful for her advice and validation.

Also, a great thanks to Miles Waggener, one of my workshop professors and a poet of kindred spirit, for taking the time to be the second reader of my thesis, his suggestions and insight on the genesis of this collection.

My poetry colleagues who I studied with at UNO, especially Cheryl Dyer, Ashley de Vries, Shukura Huggins, and Terry Belue— Thank you for being such wonderful sounding boards, as well as calming voices when I was sometime going through storms within my mind; you helped me make my way through latter semesters. Sorely, since graduation, I have missed your camaraderie.

To the fellow members of the *Gumbo Bottoms Single Pot Still Poets' Society*, especially Jon Freeland for his hard work as our first chair, and Stephen Erangey for giving poets, writers and visual artists a safe place and time to share our work and support each other on our journeys.

To the memory of my family: the decendents of Laura and Eugene, and their three daughters – Deloris, Shirley, and my mother Carolyn, who together shared the homes and responsibilities of child rearing; and to my father Wayne and his parents, Buster and Nellie, who provided a sanctuary just across the yard for a daydreamer in his younger days.

My brother, Scott, with whom I have lived a parallel life since that little pink house on the west bank of the big river. Deirdre, my cousin/sister for helping me grow into the person I am. Uncle Tommy, who is more of a brother, and has been one of my greatest friends and business partner, without whom we could not have made a success of the Pub through all these years. Paula, my baby sister/cousin for being there with me through many happy times and those few family tragedies, where we stood side by side.

My Montana family via Chicago – Brooks and Michelle Scott, and their son –my godson– Gordon Scott, for all the amazing times and conversations together over wine and whiskey, camping adventures in the north woods, dining in Chicago, encouragement, and simply being there for me over the past four decades.

All of our friends and the staff at *Paddy Malone's Irish Pub*, too many to go into here, for support and encouragement, not only with poetry, but for the past twenty-five years supporting the community we have created here together, especially Michael Johnsen, although he is Norse, has worked for us these many years as if he were family and the Irish pub were his own.

To my friends from Saverton, Ilasco, Monkey Run, and Hannibal; thanks for content for parts of these poems.

To my cousin/brotherfriend, Donald Patrick Malone; for all these years, I have missed you more than anyone will ever know.

But mostly, my deepest appreciation to my wife and partner of more than two decades, Marilee. Whenever the muse hits me or my feet start to itch with creative and/or adventurous whims, you are always at my side with reassurance and inspiration. You are the measure of my dreams.

Preface

The Ralls County Line: sketches from a rural mid-American Odyssey is a remarkable achievement. It is a powerful and elegiac collection that journeys through the landscapes of home, ancestral and otherwise. MacAllen's poems possess a clarity that is hard-earned and a music that feels both intimate and lasting. They are grounded in the daily task of living, yet they speak outward—toward history, inheritance, and the complicated ways a life is shaped by what came before it.

In these poems we enter MacAllen's Missouri and Ireland, delving into a Rural American, Gaelic and Scandinavian heritage, exploring themes of land, masculinity, ancestry, grief, and historical memory with a rare combination of lyric precision, historical aplomb and narrative richness. What strikes the reader immediately is the seriousness of this work. MacAllen's poems do not traffic in nostalgia or easy sentiment. Instead, they attend carefully to labor, weather, bodies, tools, animals, rivers, and work done over time. Meaning in this collection is cumulative rather than declarative. MacAllen trusts the pressure of detail, the repetition of image, and the persistence of voice to carry significance forward. His language is plainspoken without being plain, musical without ornament, and deeply attentive to cadence as it arises from speech, memory, and place. These poems are industrious, baptised in a work ethic both physical and spiritual, full of the everyday and the transcendent. Indeed, as Frost reminds us, and Tatman's poem enact, "the fact is the sweetest dream that labor knows."

What impresses me most about this first book is the moral and emotional intelligence of MacAllen's writing. His voice is distinctly his own—musically assured, emotionally restrained, and ethically alert. These poems understand restraint not as limitation, but as respect: respect for subject, for reader, and for the people and histories being named. He writes honestly about rural life, labor, and masculinity without romanticizing them. Strength is physical, but also brittle. Love is present, but often inarticulate. Silence speaks as loudly as affection. The poems acknowledge both endurance and cost, refusing to simplify either.

The land in this collection is not a backdrop but a presence. Rivers, hills, prairies, and fields act as witnesses and archives, carrying memory across generations. The Missouri River, in particular, becomes both literal and mythic—a force that moves commerce, labor, loss, and time itself. Tatman understands that to write about place is to write about time, and to write about time is to confront mortality. Again and again, these poems return to the question of what remains: after the work is done, after people are gone, after the seasons have passed.

Structurally, the manuscript moves with intention. Its sections—of time and place, field and stream, voyages outward and inward, kith and kin, and finally lessons learned through loss—mirror the book's central arc. This is a poetry of wandering followed by reckoning. The title poem, "The Ralls County Line," crystallizes this movement with particular force, turning a county boundary into a moral and metaphysical threshold: the line one crosses when leaving, and the line one must eventually cross over again in return. The journey outward gives the book its range; the return gives it gravity.

Formally, the poems demonstrate a confident command of line, pacing, and narrative sequence. Tatman allows poems to breathe. Long lines spool memory and history forward; calmer moments sharpen emotional focus. White space carries weight. The manuscript risks scale and intensity, but it earns that scale through discipline and revision. Each poem stands on its own while adding to a larger architecture of memory, labor, and inheritance. These poems know what they are doing, and they know why they are here.

In The Ralls County Line we encounter a true poet-historian whose work not only preserves memory but expands it. A poet whose language bears the burden of ancestry and the beauty of survival. This is a book that understands the humanity and power of attention, humility, and the courage to look closely at what we inherit—and what we carry forward when we cross the line.

\- Elizabeth A.I. Powell
Coeditor *Green Mountain Review,*
Professor of Literature & Writing
Northern Vermont University

Author's Note: Missouri vs. Missoura

For the most part, I have lost what Mark Twain called *The Pike County dialect,* his native vernacular, as well as that of Huckleberry Finn, and me. It is most likely very different in its overall sound then that of Twain's antebellum Upper Mississippi Valley maturing. I am confident that late 19th and early 20th century settlement patterns have influenced the local language in the historical Pike County expanse, from which Ralls County was formed in 1820, the year before statehood. But on occasion bits of the original speech patterns and lexicon remain and my upbringing often gives away my inherited culture.

You will observe that I use the spelling *Missoura* at times throughout this collection. My reasoning is that if you were to ever hear my poetry in my own voice, you would notice that I say the word as "muh-ZUR-uh," with both of the 'i's' being pronounced as *shwa* vowels *(uh)* and the 'ou' as a *diphthong (ur).* Growing up I never thought of this as 'controversial' – I was never corrected while in high school or when working on the tow boats- but then, at nineteen, I moved to Texas for a year and a half, before returning to the *Show Me State* to begin my college education: when my Texan acquaintances would ask where I was from, upon hearing my pronunciation, they would, to one degree or another, invariably chuckle and say, "You mean meh-ZOOR-ee." To which I would retort, "I f'ing grew up there, I think I know how the f' to say the name of my home!" – to one degree or another.

Although I recognize that the "muh-ZUR-uh" pronunciation is archaic and disappearing, I still believe this was probably the common way that the French and early American settlers said the name of the river, as well a colonial district, territory, and state. We have journals from both British and French colonial manuscripts with the spellings of *Miffoura* and *Mifsouria* in different variations, often using the long "s" spelling since the letters 's' are mid-word. In English, the letters "ia" at the end of Latin geographic names indicates a pronunciation of *ee-uh* or a diphthong of *yuh*, like *Hibernia, Caledonia, Brittania* and *Virginia*. The odd thing about the name 'Missouri' is that it first came into the English lexicon in the late 17th and mid 18th centuries at the end of the "Great Vowel Shift" which is one of the reasons (I said 'one') why Brits and Yanks have different accents. Since I seriously began researching the subject —first in Professor Tom Carneal's Missouri Folkways class at NWMSU, and then while working as a historian for Missouri State Parks— I have grown tired of having an argument every time I say the state's name. But on occasions when people are adamant to engage me on the subject, I become as obstinate as a Missoura Mule in defense of my inherited culture. (BTW, Carneal said he had pronounced the word "muh-ZUR-uh" the entirety of his raising, and he was from rural Northwest Missoura, all the way across the state from where I grew up.)

In my observation, only those from or raised in specific parts of the state say, *"muh-ZUR-uh,"* including Saverton Township in Ralls County. My late mother-in-law, Roberta, from Schuyler County up along the Iowa state line, said it that way, as does my friend Todd who grew up and lives in the greater Joplin-Neosho region down in the corner near Oklahoma and Arkansas. Of those of who use the archaic pronunciation, our numbers grow fewer every day, because of collectivized education's narrow minded tenacious defense of the Puritanical rule of blindly using the long 'ee' ending, without even looking for historic evidential support. And the influences of internet, radio, television have taken their toll, especially the recent epidemic of arrogant and annoying Sports Book app advertisers who have celebrities and athletes pronouncing the name as *"Meh-ZOOOR-EE"* (the middle syllable rhyming with 'sewer'). In a hundred years, if the world doesn't blow up or mankind isn't wiped out in an epidemic and outside cultural pressures continue, that only pronunciation known within our borders will sound like someone from New Jersey with an adenoid condition.

However you say it, I really don't care. I won't correct anyone or proselytize to turn them toward the truth; I don't have to. It's not their fault, being raised by the heathen and that's all they've ever known. If you are so inclined to know my academic justification for the usage of said admittedly archaic pronunciation, I have published an essay on my Substack page for your perusal, if you are curious and openminded. *judemacallen.substack.com*

"I have no respect for a man who can spell a wurd only one way."

      -Sam Clemans (attributed)

Table of Contents:

for Marilee –

I.

Of Time and Place

...out back

near the corner posts of the abandoned corral,
beside a large thriving vegetable garden planted
thru four generations and still tilled,
there is an old empty wellhouse beneath
the ground—
The one that the big sorrel gelding,
Romeo, slipped down into
when he stepped on the sheet metal
and boards that bent and splintered
under his massive hooves
—it is still there, buried,
unused, no water drawn
from it for a half a century
on, should have been
filled in and forgotten
once the Old Man rescued
that huge gentle horse,
uninjured by his misfortune.
          Dad said when he found
the chestnut big boy in that dilemma
—his blonde forelocks and white blazed
head calmly sticking out of the hole—
he was certain he'd have to shoot
the poor thing, cut him into pieces
to get him out of the hole; then he sat down
on a stump of firewood and smoked a Winston,
working it out in his mind how a man

could get a half-ton and more of horse
up and out of a below-ground concrete
box.
      The wellhouse is still there. Surrounded
by fencing, needing to be filled in
with dirt or sand decades ago—
I reckon it's still there
because of my family's love
of old stories.

The Ancient Hill

I climbed atop of the ancient hill,
that stood sentinel over the valley
of my youth and dreams,
carved from limestone and shale
by a legendary river before, during,
and after the great glaciers scoured
down from the north over forty thousand
years, burnishing layers of earth spread
by primordial seas two-hundred million years
ago, over bedrock of granite and rhyolite
lifted a billion years before by St. Francois intrusion
creating the oldest mountains in North America
to rise amid the Ozarks pushing the course
of the great waterway to sculpt the border
between the American West and East, the future
and the past, the river cutting through dirt and rock
and till laid down, grinding the gravel from paleo seas,
exposing volcanic foundations arisen—
all washed away over another
forty million years to form the valley
of my childhood,
my father's childhood,
my grandfather's homestead.

I looked down from the summit
on my brother's little pink house
which stood among the homes

of my parents and grandparents,
where we once waited for Christmas
mornings and school buses as yellow
leaved sycamores and cottonwood shone
with scarlet maples spread through the bottoms,
while on the hills– the battered knuckle bones
of the geological ages past –the colors of dun
    and orange
from the dried and dying leaves of hickory and oak
curled and crumbled before spinning down amongst
sparse patches of rusty red cedars spread through
grey stands of ironwood, dogwood, and ash on
    the ridges,
all blanketing the land like a bright Missoura
    made quilt
in the long warm sunbeams of an Autumnal afternoon,
where blue tick hounds dozed, bird dogs lazed, horses
    grazed,
old men lied about fishing, old women gossiped about
    old men,
and that big river flowed on, like time, going, here
    then gone.

One morning while on a sojourn in West Texas
a dream nearly slipped by
behind my eyes just before dawn,
the sun hit an early red dust sky
as echoing thunderheads distantly roared
with sanguine rain falling like a sacrifice,
bleeding into my eyes and through that wounded

veil I saw those mansions of emerald leaves thriving
in mid-Summer of youth, camping on sand bars,
running bank and trot lines, catching fish, building
memories around bonfires, telling stories
and half lies and laughing in the dark until dawn,
waking to a sun rising on the Illinois side
and limestone bluffs gleaming upon the ancient hill
above that ever-running river wide—
and wiping the blood from my eyes I awakened to find
    time
growing short that morning in Texas with my boots
still upon the *Llano Estacado,*
Coronado's sea of grass
so far and wide.

My visits are frequent now since nearer to home,
yet this world calls like a siren to lead me toward rocks
so sheer. The promise of treasure is great, yet delivery
fleeting— failure is always a risk when fishing
for fortune—
I return to hike to the summit of our ancient hill
and look down upon what was left to me,
by men and women who came before,
who built their own houses
with muscle and sweat and took care
of their own—
my birthright, that I have left
in the care of my brother,
who tends to the sanctuary
of Christmas mornings
yet to come.

Sink or Swim: Ch. 2, 1979

Wished the years away
thru twelve grades, now anxious
to walk that march in red robe
and miter board; get it over with!
What's the big fucking deal?
Come Monday, I'm still
working on the dock
at the grain terminal,
probing beans and corn
moving from part-time
up to full time
with winter wheat harvest
and eventually someday,
my mother had been told,
(and she proudly passed
the news on to me)
Assistant Grain Inspector,
if I wanted it. But, I didn't—

The Old Man had made it clear;
there are those who are born
and the world waits on them
hand and foot.

We are not they.
We are those
who fix our own breakfast,

take our lunch to work,
put supper on the table,
cut our grass,
mow other people's lawns,
change our oil,
learn shade tree mechanics,
grow gardens for food
not flowers,
raise chickens to sell
fryers and eggs,
butcher our own
beef and hogs,
cut firewood in the winter,
sell seasoned firewood come fall,
have woodstoves not fireplaces,

save what we can, do what we must,
keep on living.

It was time to sink or swim, he told me.
Same as He said when I was seven;
my brother and I donned Mae West
lifejackets before he began to toss us
from the jon boat up into the fading
lavender light of a summer night
to splash down just upstream
into the Mississippi's swirling
opaque dark green current, while he sat
in the stern, smiling, smoking a Muriel,
barking commands like a laughing drill sergeant:

KICK WITH YOUR LEGS!
PULL WITH YOUR ARMS!
C'MON! SWIM,
GODDAMNIT!

And a decade on,
standing in the dusty drive before
his garage, my Tony Lama's crunching
nervously on creek rock gravel as if
walking on the broken glass of living
eighteen years beneath his roof,
his Nordic blue eyes
piercing like glacial ice
staring into mine
of Irish hazel grey;

Boy, grow up. Figure it out!
Because fucking around
here, playing baseball and
drinking beer, isn't a life,
or a career.

He then turned his back to me, walked away, wiping
the oil from his weather-beaten hands
with a faded well-worn red shop rag,
returning to his labors, just
as he did everyday
of his life.

Eels

Writhing
        wriggling
                mass,
dead-eyed black slick olive gray
rolling ribbons of tubular muscle—
confined within the fish trap,
the swarm's slime displaces
water held within the staves
of the well-crafted oak box.
My father curses. *Goddamnit!*
Flips the latch,
        drops the door,
                dumps them out—
Nasty sonsofbitches, he swears,
shaking the muck
from his hand.

Fascinated, I study
their Sargasso Sea shimmy
as they slither down
into the darkness, off into
the Mississippi River's
forever flow.

The waiter at *Love Sushi* asks;
What you like?
        Unagi, please, I say,
        with a knowing smile.

Winter's Edge

Once I welcomed Winter's edge with its keen
quick cuts from northwest gusts sharp as honed
steel blades slicing across deeply drifted snow
silenced hills & iced over Salt River with skiffs
skittering across the hard grey surface & above
on bluff tops the dark twisted tracery branches
of hardwoods stood as stark sentinels against
an inviolate midwinter's sky as blue
as my grandfather's watery eyes same
as I saw in my father's visage same as
I know of my brother when he gazes back
remembering the land and times together all
those frozen days felling trees cutting firewood
ceasing only for sips of steaming coffee black
& to abundantly breathe of the freezing firmament
of rime & ice down from a boreal world
of once Ancient Stone Gods of fire & ice
stoicism & sagas of our Nordic ancestors
who dwelt in that realm of long harsh bitter cold—
we –like they– accepted fate without complaint
for life could always be worse & inhaled deeply
thankfully of that fresh frigid affirming sacrament
together as a low winter sun sank
soft & early from a paling sky fading to purple
puce & pink beyond those very certain hills
known well & when closing my eyes they
are always there when my lungs were young

& strong before these knees & knuckles creaked
cracked when we stacked those hard-earned logs
& sticks carefully in neat racks & ricks to season
before the next winter to be split to fit in stoves
that warmed babies & mamas fathers & sons
in hand-built cabins & houses
where we kept shelter.

The Patron

In latest of afternoons or earliest of evenings,
with hangover cleared and stomach settled,
he'd walk alone five blocks down to the pub
and take a seat upon his regular barstool
at the far end of the bar, facing the door.

Nary a word before a mug of Falstaff appeared
on the polished counter; the old bar and back bar
a matched set, brought upriver from New Orleans
on steamboat in 1903, when the tavern was established.
He came here as a boy, with his granddad and uncles,
had his first whiskey right where he sat. He was fifteen,
the night his Pops passed, away— and but for that
    stint
in Vietnam, he was one of the first in, Army combat
construction engineers, and lucky to be one of the
    first ones
out— he'd have drunk there, and been drunk there,
    nearly
every night, but for Sunday Blue Laws, fucking pain
    in the ass.
Fucking religion. He'd lost any need for priests,
or parish, many years before, at *Ia Drang.*

Shortly after the draft beer arrived, the barman came
    forth
with an ample pour of Bourbon, neat, in a squat
    glass tumbler

on the side, with a smile, nod, and fresh bowl of pretzels
or dry roasted peanuts. Slowly, with the heavy and once
    agile
now arthritic fingers of a retired ironworker, he'd spin
    his drink
in the dim glow of the antique lamps, watching the
    light's
refraction dance through the bevels and amber
    liquescence,
as he tried not to dwell upon the last eleven winters
and the lost seasons between, while the juke box played
Patsy, Hank Sr., Johnny Cash, Buddy Holly, Waylon and
    Willie
crooned, drifting above the underlying aromas
of stale beer and bleach.

He finished the whiskey first and second; the bartender
    always
quick with the pours, no need to ask. The Falstaff—
    an old man's
brand few bars still had on a handle —always lasted
    longer than
the Ten High. With each drink delivered he'd slide
    another buck
from the stack of bills beside the heavy tawny glass
    ashtray.
He tipped extra to a fault, sometimes two bucks a beer
so they'd take care of him. They earned it. He sure as
    fuck
wasn't saving it for anyone's goddamned inheritance.

The damn kids; one in Chicago, two in Houston,
never saw them anymore. Since the funeral
they haven't even been back home. Fuck 'em.
But these kids here at the bar, they watched out for me.
And the money? It'd never all be spent —she rat-holed
so much cash behind my back: Old Judge coffee cans
and Ball mason jars crammed full in the closet behind
     hat boxes,
in the cellar with old, canned goods, up in the rafters
      in the attic.
Gotta call Hickman, the lawyer, get my final will and
      testament
figured out, so it goes to these kids here, sure not leave it
for them fuckin'ingrates to fight over in probate.

As the evening slipped away, he'd buy rounds
for the bar, whether stranger, friends or old foes:
it was time to forgive, while yearning
to forget.

Sometime after smoking his last Camel, he'd buy a
      new pack for home,
while the crowd was growing younger, louder,
      the juke box calling up
the Talking Heads, Bowie, The Boss, Fleetwood Mac,
      ELO, Supertramp
and other noises only tolerated until he'd drunk
      enough to lightly numb
the longing. One of the bartenders would help him
      stagger up Bird Street

to an empty house, get him settled, say goodnight,
    see ya tomorrow.

He'd pour a nightcap into one of her Waterford snifters,
admire the golden light from the mica-shaded lamps
reflecting through the cut crystal clear years,
and he'd smile— if for just a moment—
raise a glass, to his Sharon, always hoping, he might
see her, though doubtful, again.

Lighting one more cigarette, he'd drunkenly fall back
into a threadbare recliner beside the plastic-wrapped
    Davenport.
Then faintly, he'd drift off to the drone of the ten
    o'clock news,
before Carson came on, as a cigarette smoldered
    between his fingers,
as he drifted away to a life where he wouldn't wake
to another morning without her.

Tattoo

Often, I am asked —*and No, I don't*—
though on odd occasions perhaps
have pondered but always
revoked by that singular recollection
of the once seen never unseeable
image of an inky muddled woman
performing the act of fellatio forever
emblazoned on the forearm of a man
I loved as I have never loved
anyone from childhood to this day.
He also wore the sinful brand
of *"Ruby Harrigan"* on his shoulder—
not my grandmother's name
—for the entirety of their fifty-five years
they shared a bed, ate meals together
at that small kitchen table where
I would always find them drinking coffee
or playing pinochle with their friends,
and never a word spoken by anyone
regarding the tattoos in front of us,
until death they did part.

My grandfather
— I can never forget how he wept
every day of three years
from grandma's death
until his own—

perhaps unspoken guilt and loss
never assuaged in the face
of the permanence of stain.

Joey

"Death steals everything except our stories."
                                    - Jim Harrison,

January, when the creek iced over solid
You would ride that red rusted junk bike
down the sand hill, the clay and dirt frozen hard,
speeding up, flying into the air over to the far bank
tumbling crashing across the gravel bar, popping up
with the laughter of an insane acrobat.
Bruises, scrapes, scratches, cuts; seems you never
walked away unscathed, trips to the emergency room,
once for thirteen stitches on the right brow,
        another time
found you limping home after breaking the little bone
in your left leg. The rest of us were chickenshits;
we'd only make the run when it was soft
and sandy, tires sinking into the muck
we'd never get enough steam built up before
hitting the plywood and earthen berm,
and we'd roll ass over tea kettle,
splashdown in the creek, soaking
wet, yet- for the most part -uninjured.

You rode horses with the same recklessness;
bareback— while the rest of us saddled up.
"Like the Osage!" you'd cry just before the fall
from the back of that twitchy pinto mare, hard
to the ground of April when showers
would somewhat temper the dirt and hurt.

It was in August—
I was saddling the sorrel gelding when mom came to
    tell me;
You'd been thrown from the back of a brahma bull,
gored on decent, then tossed up into the heat
of an Alabama night, landing hard on the dry arena
    floor,
stomped on by cloven hooves. Your heart was crushed,
the blood spilling onto the red clay ground.

After forty-one years I plainly see
no one truly gets over anything, especially
seeing You – soaring on a crimson Western Flyer
over a frozen creek, high across the clearest
of winter skies.

Saint Elizabeth

—for Carolyn

"All thinking men are atheists."

—Ernest Hemingway, A Farewell to Arms

You–
Mother of *The Baptiste*–
your nuns held me wrapped in a blanket
once released unto this world from my own
mother's embrace.
her first born,

or so they tell me.
I don't remember it all.
I suppose I'll take their word for it.

They later taught me that
You lost your husband, Zachariah,
into the hands of Herod the Great—
whose men carved him down in the temple
because he would not give over
Your only begotten Son,
concealed from the
        (absolutely unfounded)
 'Slaughtering of the Innocents,'
 saving *The Baptiste,*
Your only Son, upon which so much of this story
is dependent. Our sacred mythology
wouldn't remain if not for

You—
Mother of *The Baptiste*—
and Your Son who cleansed
your cousin

       (or was he your great nephew?)
the *Lamb of God*, whom he bathed
in the River Jordan, washed away
his sins, as we must all have them
washed away, purged from our souls,
those we have yet to commit
and those left upon us by Adam and Eve,
and the serpent's seduction.
it is only by Your Son—
The Baptiste
—that we are saved from the vile taint
of conception in sin,
of being born.
You—
Mother of *The Baptiste*—
gave over Your only Son, not of your own behest,
   I assume

       (or did God tell you that
       This too shall come to pass?)
His head placed on a platter
for the amusement of a girl, a child,
the Princess Salome, granddaughter
       (or was she a stepdaughter?
depends on who you read.)
of Herod Antipas, a madman,
Roman puppet who called himself king,

cared not to be criticized, called out
for adultery by a zealot living wild,
among nature, with God in the wilderness.
Herod caged Your Son —*The Baptiste*—
then slaughtered him, just as his father
had been slaughtered, You remained
alone for the rest of the story, negligently
left out for the rest of Your life by
a council in Nicaea. Regardless
of what was done to Your Great Nephew
(or is he a cousin?) The Savior,
the Lamb of God,
Christos,
Moshiach—
the hate of the House of Herod
was undeniably the cruelest toward
You.

I've pondered often, sometimes hands folded,
other times they held a glass of wine—
how would the story play out had
Your Son– *The Baptiste* – survived?
Very different I'm certain,
especially the sacrament of communion,
given that the Father above forbade
The Baptiste of taking fermented drink
(or so he said). Or perhaps not; it wouldn't
be wine once it was said to be the blood
of Christ, the Savior, the Redeemer
now, would it? Perhaps, Your Son,
 The Baptiste,

would not have approved, and then to hell with history
–Avignon, Martin Luther, Calvin, Henry VIII–
this rebel cult of Judaism may have split
right at the very beginning.
And where would that have left the rest of it?
With *Mithras, Zeus, Jupiter,* or *Odin* above
to petition in our hour of need?

But what do I know? Being just an unlearned sinner,
a heathen taught to read, these trivial thoughts,
a young priest once told me it matters not.
It is Faith in the unknowable mysteries
that promises eternal life; questioning,
and curiosity, he instructed, *has led many*
a soul to purgation.

But there is one thing I know
that is a certainty in this story—
tragically, God asked very much of
You–
Mother of *The Baptiste*–
How much can a mother's love endure?
You gave up immeasurably—
Your Husband, Your Only Child,
Your Life–
without a thought of Yourself? for what?
a few lines by Luke in his book,
yet nothing from Matthew, Mark,
let alone John.
But You–

did get a hospital in Hannibal
named in Your honor, whereas
on an early July morning,
a young woman gave birth to a boy,
and two and a half decades later,
one sweltering July evening,
there that same boy died
– for just a moment –
in Your emergency room, frothy blood
from a ruptured lung poured forth,
ribs broken; heart bruised— not by a woman
but by a burly shortstop, from a collision
in shallow leftfield, heart stopped,
world spinning, the veil descended, life
had paused–

Then I was resurrected
in intensive care, for the next three days,
would live, be fine, and I laughed;
I caught the ball, I told my mother,
who in that moment, was not amused
with any gallows humor.

After a day and a half at my bedside
Doc Waltersheid convinced her to go
home, get some rest, everything
was going to be alright – and I was.
Resilience was my one boon,
one of my few God-given
blessings.

It was just before dawn, in those hours
when they said I was born
twenty-five years before,
the lights were dimmed through the halls,
Monitors beeped softly in the rhythmic cadence
of a beating heart, and there I saw

You—
Mother of *The Baptiste*—
standing at the foot of my bed,
draped in sackcloth and ashes,
Your nephew
      (or is he your cousin?)
nailed to his tree upon the wall
behind your calm soft face;
I shuddered.
      Have you come for me?
      How did you give so much?
      and for what?
      Tell me— did it really matter?
      Did any of it really happen, at all?

You answered not, nodded to me,
and somewhere I heard a gentle voice,
from within—

      "Seek."

and you turned, fading away
on the third day
in the dimly lit morning.

It might have been the morphine in my blood,
or the codeine behind my eyes,
perhaps the concussion
on the back of my head, or perhaps
the power of persuasion,
a Mother's Love, or maybe
a dose of each.

I still ponder these things,
seeking those truths I know
will never be found.
I wasn't there – Neither
were any other first-hand witnesses
to tell these truths. Who knows?
Only the dead are certain
of the veracity of all latter day
historians and prophets telling the tales
to fit their needs, or the government's
needs, emperors, tsars, kaisers, kings,
presidents and prime ministers, but
what do I know?

Being the faithless miseducated skeptic
(going to hell, or purgatory, if i am lucky)
that I am.

I suppose
I'll have to take their word for it.
I wasn't there at all.

On Warm Days in Winter

-for Jeff "not the Dude" Bridges

On warm days in winter with unbroken skies
warmed by easy southwest breezes sweeping across
lately cut corn fields, sunbeams gleaming through
leafless branches of hardwoods, their twisted shade
settling dark upon dried grasses grown knee-deep
around edges of old pastures where horses stood
grazing long-shadowed in the afternoon,
with their rough shaggy coats warm
in the slanted chromatic light
of those perfect days between Christmas
and New Year's when we were both back home—

You on leave, I was on break— we tramped
up old traces into the bluff tops where the dogs
ran unencumbered through woods and clearings
We talked of the history of this place— our place
—so it would remain in the memory of the wind:
Joliet and Marquette, Pontiac, Boone and Clark,
Zebulon Pike, Tecumseh, Black Hawk—
how their canoes and bateaux voyaged,
moccasins tread, horses trod past
where we now stood in awe to talk
of growing up in a valley where great ghosts
had once worked, labored, fought, and fell,
leaving their sweat, spit, blood
beneath our footsteps

while above and before us we beheld boundless
blue skies reflecting on the wide tableau
of our forever flowing river, never to think
on days ahead when all things
for us too might end.

The Coyotes of Covid

in memory of Kodi. 2012-2023

> *He died too soon, as good dogs do.*
> *I naively wished we could have grown*
> *old together.*

Sitting in the darkness of earliest morning,
I throw another stick of seasoned maple on the
    crackling
fire holding off the damp chill. I sip on single pot still,
counting cars, listening to the oddly long minutes
    between
the crossings of sedans, pickups, long-haul truckers,
their wheels hissing, motors rumbling humming
and screaming as they cross over the wide River
    Missoura;
the world isn't dead—— not yet,
but it's obviously sick, and scared.

Layer upon layer of fog rises from the warm water
as blankets of cool clear night air spreads across
the surface flowing. The murkiness climbs, enshrouds
the bridge until all that is seen are dim lights
blinking red and green marking port and starboard
for passage between the piers, with the constant amber
fuzz of sodium lights along the outline of steel
    superstructure,
with the sporadic shadow of a Ford, a Chevy, or Subaru
jellybean shaped SUV, its low beams and flood lamps
scurrying off somewhere to hide.

As ever faithful, Kodí lies to my left,
resting his heavy right flank alongside
my chair, his paw always touching my foot.
He raises his head— staring into the misty shade
like a great hound guarding a manor on the moors,
he warns with guttural growls just— before
— yes, I hear them, too; the howls, the yips, the yowls
of rampant excitement. He wails a long guttural
sound back at them, and they stop their singing,
puzzled with the deep Labrador baritone voice,
warning his very distant cousins to stay away.

With humans quarantined,
life for the resident coyotes has expanded,
the territories and hours of operation
for *canis latrans* have widened far beyond
normal river bottom woods and field haunts,
as they have crossed the river by pedestrian bridge,
they are no longer down along the tracks, they are up
from Adrian's Island, onto West Main Street, feasting
from the dumpster at Arris's Pizza Palace, walking
thru the capitol grounds, perhaps soon
inside the capitol itself, brazenly,
as if they owned the world, as habitants
of seats of government are most often
known to do.

It is hard to be certain where these prairie wolves
will go with their newfound freedom and power,
given this surrounding shadowy stillness
that has settled over the land.

These thoughts have me prophetic and pleased—
If all of mankind dies within the next few weeks
or months perhaps
a new life might be better
for another apex predator.

Nightsongs

Before the commonality of air-conditioning,
lying in the darkness of that corner room,
awake, sweating, the windows open
hoping for the slightest breeze to stir
heavy air away from saturated skin,
as the sounds of the deep night surged
up from the shadowed haunts
of the river bottoms—

Barred owls with their melancholy trills
calling "helloo? where are you?"
and their cousin screech owls shrieked
the drowsing away until i learned
to love their frightful song in the gloom.
a bobcat, for whom silence is survival,
sometimes screamed frighteningly close,
chilling my blood, keeping me awake
for a week in hopes of being terrified
once more by her caterwauling –all of this
operatic singing above the symphony
of incessant droning
on a bed of bullfrogs bellowing,
tree frogs croaking,
cicadas clicking,
crickets chirping—
a chorus of nightly lullabies
from the familiar woods and thickets.

i would fight the sleep from coming
in at the corner of my eyes, waiting
to hear the first sounds of a midnight train
down through Keokuk, then Hannibal
headed south to cross the Mississippi at Alton,
on to Cairo and over the Ohio
down to Memphis bound for New Orleans,
always sounding those two loud blasts
of the horn from the Saverton general store
confirming my awareness of place
in geography along the big river, before
another blast of the horn at the bridge
over our creek just behind the house
telling us where we all belonged.

the rambling diesel locomotives bellowing
the all-encompassing mechanical meter and rhyme
filling the night, i could feel the rattling and rolling
of steel wheels singing on the rails,
the cars laden with ore, grain, and coal
rocking to and fro, the ties shuddering
down into the levee, up into the bank,
shaking the foundations of our home
and my bones until it continued on,
another blast of the horn trailing
off toward the crossing of Salt River,
the click and clack of the caboose
fading away, gone, and
there was, for a moment,
silence—

just before
a horse nickers in the corral while
a lone whip-poor-will wistfully
warbles from a hollow sycamore
at the edge of the woods, and far across
Jim Thompson's fields of tall corn
come the yelps and yowls
of the coyotes' howls—
arias at the foot of the hills
to remind us –
they were always there.

II.

Of Fields and Streams

Renewal

we wait all winter
through dark nights until finally
staying up for dawn's first light
as the steam from my coffee cup
and on our breath hangs baited briefly
above the backyard while the first
of a blood orange dawn rises over the river
bearing witness to my deferred happiness
at seeing the joy of this brace of bird dogs
when first they hear the waterfowl returning
from their winter interval. Dogs run
as far as the fence separating us from bluff's edge
allows or they would consider
leaping into oblivion— instead
they freeze with the hardened gaze of statues
their tails straight and stiffly quivering
one front paw slightly lifted from the turf
pointing at the flocks flying over the river
coming to land in the marshy spring flooded fields
of Callaway County where the ducks and geese yield
resting on their long passage north with spring
moonrise on their right wing genetically embedded
upon their being— foraging flapping squawking honking
—in the soft suffused mist of an early Missoura morning.

my doctor warns not to drink coffee
night and day to stay up all hours
for this ritual at my age
but the years are now
burning away
like the murky fog
beneath the burning sun
as time goes on—
on until it's gone
and at this point in the story
I can't really see
any further harm
being done.

Angling

Despite being sore and aged,
this poorly repaired—
before being damaged again
—shoulder, clumsily still
can cast a wooly bugger
yellow and brown, landing
in the slack of an eddy
just beneath a shallow shoal.
Slowly, stripping back the line,
a few inches at a time, when—
a spot rolls on the surface ever
so slightly, the fly is taken, the pull on the line,
brought tightly, raise the rod tip high to the right,
guide the running fish, a goggle eye, through the waters
blue green of the Gasconade, lead it away from
    the flow,
up toward my hand, its bronze mottled spines, fins,
    slab sides
gleam in the sunlight, the fish gently taken by the jaw,
the hook is slipped from the upper lip, with respect,
admire this saucer sized fighter, her red moon-eyed
    glare,
kneel easily with care let her loose from capture
into the stream, she swiftly spins away goes deep
into the pool like all the other panfish
who have taken my fly in this mottled
afternoon light, they live to fight
another day.

Great blue heron flies in low to the water, spreading
    its wings,
lands on spindly legs in a patch of watercress
    downstream
at the mouth of a spring. I will leave him the river
    for a while,
reel my line in, walk up the bank, away to camp,
with no fish to clean,
happily, okay.

Dove Season

*"I'd be happy to have my biography be the stories of my dogs. To
me, to live without dogs would mean accepting a form of blindness."*

-Thomas McGuane

With a flutter and flurry
of gray and white feathers
scattered in a clear blue sky—
a brace of bird dogs bolts toward the quarry,
the dove tumbles from the air like an elusive fly ball
dying just beyond a shortstop's reach in a shallow
    leftfield
of corn stubble—
girl dog gets there first, with a snatch,
quick and careful, she carries the carcass in her soft
    pink mouth,
turns proud in a gallop as her younger brother runs at
    her side
playfully bedevils her with nips yips yowls growls all
    the way
back to where she places her trophy into the hand of
    their human,
who smiles, kneels to give both benedictions,
and rewards— brisk rub on their necks
just below the ears, they smile with tongues
lolling out the side of their mouths,
panting, eyes closed, muzzles held high,

elated in hearing their names—
Good girl, Fiona.
Good Boy, Seamus.
Good dogs.
Good good dogs.

Rise

Sluggishly,
with the grace
of a fat beaver, or
an alligator snapping turtle,
that crawls up from the river to
sun upon a mud bank or dried log

I rise
into this day
of black coffee,
Jimmy Buffet ballads,
curmudgeonly cats, and noble dogs
who warm this house in ways
only good gods could grant.

At the Mouth of the Osage

I.
The gentle Osage flows flat this evening;
the raucous Missoura draws it in,
the big river rolling on like an army
of endless time pulling the past
and peace away.

Standing witness to this union, I painfully
watch your lovely azure green waters
born beyond the Ozark hills running smoothly
until they merge with the opaque brown deluge
carrying silt from the Great Plains thunderstorms
and like an arranged marriage of a sweet maiden
from the hills to a powerful scion of the prairie
who sweeps her swiftly away to far off
industrial destinations —St. Louis,
Memphis, Natchez, New Orleans.

Sunlight wanes as a waxing moon grows above
the horizon, creeping up from behind the hills
of *Cote Sans Dessein* where ghosts
of *trappeurs et voyageurs perdus*
gather in the twilight wondering how,
since it is said spirits cannot cross waters
can they ever return to their sanctified grounds
of *Quebec et Louisianne?*

II.
Jefferson sent men to discover you, though
you were already well known to many nations.
Lewis & Clark camped at your point of confluence.
Pike ascended your flow to meet the people
who gave their name to your waters, humans
of dignity, tall handsome bison hunters on
the edge of hills and plains,
the edge of legend and history,
the edge of tradition and technology,
who like their river had rode and run
free for as long as the hills had been alive
until the white man's engineers came
with steamrollers to crush the antiquated
bucolic backward beauty— they thought
you better harnessed, shackled, impounded,
damned.
I dream of what your wild ways were when gazing
over these lands once so rugged, raw, Jefferson's frontier
to last a thousand years; but an unbound bomb
of modernity, massacre, and manifest destiny exploded,
with steel plows from a man named Deere, with
an arsenal filled by men named Sharp,
Winchester, Remington, Browning, Gatling,
and Colt, carried destruction on steel arteries
across the land, they talked on singing lines
that were strung across the skies; there was no fighting
it once industry took over. Within a hundred years
from the time that keel boatmen pulled their vessels
upstream with cordage heavy over shoulders

legs pumping in the quicksand and muck past your
open mouth, just before steamships were crossing
the Atlantic in days, not weeks, and two brothers
at Kittyhawk had soared across the sky. How could
    you
have had any hope in the face of an enemy so alien
to your world? With the power of a poured concrete
    noose
across your spine, constricting your beautiful feral
    flow,
tamed one day in the future
when human frailty is eventually exposed;
dams will break and walls will fall.
Time ends all things, especially the best laid
plans, only our lives are too short to know
this is already over.

III.
Wistfully wishing I could fold back this tableau
of time so I might travel, powered by paddle over
canoe routes of the *Wazahaze* and *Coureur du Bois*
who followed the traces of woodland bison
turned to the moccasin paths of the long hunters—
the channels of the keel boatmen—
the horse trails and fords of the Rangers —
Boone, Callaway, Cole, McNair—
afore axe blades of lumbermen stripped your hills
    bare—
afore picks of miners delved deep into your bed—
afore settlers burned your canebrakes dead—

afore lumber roads became highways and lakes flooded
with behemoth boats roaring over and over and over,
    forever
lost are primeval nights where once was heard
only the call of barred owls, red wolves lonely howls
through your hollows, over those hills, with the dusky
    songs
of whippoorwills and cardinal's trills to greet the dawn
    awakening
your Missoura morn, long before you were my *belle*
    rivière

IV.
Dusk now, nearly dark, fireflies
hang over the glade, heat lightning flashes
beyond the clouds hanging distantly on emerging Mars
glowing angry red over the horizon. I gaze north, past
    the point
where two waters become one, both are now dark as
    unrecalled
dreams. Polaris twinkles bright above and the moon full
    floods
its beams upon your calm water as the last rays of the
    sun paint
pastels of pink and violet beyond the western hills.

Turning away with a whistle for the dogs
to load into the Jeep, the top down,
our summer treat,
drive home in this twilight,

looking back in the review mirror
on your flow and I know, longing over those currents
coming together, running away, taking my days.
Wistful, woeful, wonderful, willing to come
here again, before my history is over and told.
I have grown too old
       to paddle your waters alone
       longing for the solitude
       of being carried upon
       your back.

Phases of the Moon

With full moons coming faster for me now
since sunsets are growing fewer. I know
twenty-eight days still are only four weeks,
but every twenty-four hours slips off
like another thief into the shadows
taking with it what little that's left
of the calendar and clock.

I'd be but nine seasons old if I were just a hound.
My last three pups all died before they reached
thirteen. We once sang at the moon while camped
along the river, bonfires blazing, embers dancing
above flowing waters as vees of autumn snow geese
honked in their flight through the lunar light
on pathways written on maps of their very being;
moonrise at the left wing in October,
on the right at winter's end.

Lake sturgeon—calm, pale, gigantic,
some more than eight feet long, growing
to an eighth of a ton, returned
to the clear running Osage again,
spawning, living, thriving, even at my age
they still have yet a half more life to survive.
There is an old fish, older than I will ever see,
who feels *la clair de lune* of a thousand months
shining down through the rippled watery surface

on its ancient bony armor scaled back before
it will leave its ghost to the deep, crossing over
into the night of dark water's ceaseless course.

Since before we were homo erectus, howling hounds,
flying fowl, or swimming schools of spawn,
we gazed up at the pallid, lustrous orb
of the night, as the light hides our truer
side, we are soft in the shadows away
from fright, can't be spied by monsters
of sight in their haunts of daylight.
Safe are we, creatures longing
for shelter beneath her phases.

The Persimmon Trees

There were a pair of persimmon trees on a gentle slope
of open pasture at the mouth of Cameron Creek hollow
near the edge of the Eichenberger's place where the
    cattle
kept the greenest of grass grazed so close and clean it
    gleamed
in the dimming evenings as we hiked out of the dark
Oko Tipi hills coming in from hunting elusive and
    fleeting
morel mushrooms in the musty leaf litter
of the hardwoods' spring.

A female and a male persimmon tree standing
in a verdant field together, alone, separate from the rest
of the trees in the woods.

In autumn when we'd walk along the creek, the dogs
hoping to scare up squirrels, the trees bearing fruit,
    orange yellow
turning dark, tasty treats for crows, deer, possums,
    raccoons,
and even us, if we could harvest them in time.

We'd fill our pockets with fruit, sit beneath the trees
and feast, tossing away the hard un-ripened bitter ones,
as well as those grown too old, rotten and ruined,
but choosing only those with skin supple, and flesh soft,

creamy, sweet, as all we creatures love them best,
and we'd daydream, together, until dusk began to fall
and the moonrise over the river shone bright upon
the pasture grass so we could see to make our way
back down the road home in the dimming of the day.

Seas of Corn

In the depths of summer, the hills and draws
above the Nodaway and Nishnabotna rivers
undulate like seas of corn, washing
in waves across Iowa to spill onto
the shores of northern Missoura.

We have cornfields in our state but nothing
compared to those of our neighbors to the north.
They go on forever up there, like the Labrador Sea
between Qaqortoq and L'Anse aux Meadows,
those unforgiving leagues of Leif Erikson's
voyages, roughly rolling waters
that only Vikings could endure,
while hauling on frozen ropes,
pulling oars in an open boat
below battered sails,
soaring up and over,
diving down between
mammoth swells
into deep drowning troughs.

Scandinavian immigrants, descendants
of those stalwart Vikings, arrived
on these shores, braved vast rolling prairies
and the wide plains of the upper Midwest,
after crossing the North Atlantic in the belly
of a boat, trekking half a continent with their lives
carried upon weary backs—

they effortlessly brushed a few low hills off
their tired shoulders as if easily wiping
so much dust and sweat from their brow
with ragged handkerchiefs,
spitting on blistered bleeding hands,
that guided dour draught horses pulling
steel ploughs through unturned virgin soil,
cutting the land into acres and sections, sowing seeds,
creating those great inland seas of corn, wheat, barley,
    and beans,
feeding a nation, feeding the world, writing another
    checkered chapter
in the American tale.

Naiads

In the right kind of quiet, I hear soft rivers
running— deep through my veins,
whispering beneath the clutter of life,
in dreams siren voices of nymphs
come washing through time
and memories, they sing
their spirits names flow
downstream
      —Mississippi,
        Missouri,
          Cuivre,
            Current,
              Gasconade,
                Big Piney,
                  Niangua,
                    Meramec—

I am enthralled, captivated by their call,
reminded of enduring baptisms.

But only when at home
do I feel their seductive flow—
just as Hylas was pulled into Pagea
—they reach out for me, grasping
from gumbo bottoms, rising from
hollows into limestone bluffs, leaching
up through oak floorboards, climbing

into our bluff top bungalow, seeping
up through the dark rich earth, feeding
my brother's garden, soaking
up through my bare feet, merging
into my battered legs, rushing
through old bones, strumming
the fibers around my heart,
mending muscles, calming
frayed nerves—
  I am soothed...
  haunted.

The Last of November

Low run the rivers at the last of November,
   geese fly southward on paths well remembered
   as lost leaves of sycamores softly descended
   through bare bleached branches at autumn's surrender
   when we found quail with the coming of winter
   along the edge of cut fields and old pastures
   as black and liver flecked English Setters
   pointed birds in the brush where
   the spring creek meanders
   below stands of red cedars
   rusty and verdant above
   on the ridge.

The Old Man never missed
   with that Belgian-made Browning;
   the sixteen gauge. He sold that gun
   when he was dying,
   his very last November.

Someday, I must tell him about these
   Wirehaired Griffons we have now,
   such good bird dogs.
He'd be proud.

Alone with the River

alone with the river
i look out on December's day
as the last of snow geese fly away

through cloudbank skies
of dark gunmetal gray
as the sun slips down

into the gloaming
with the nightfall descending
before the light vanishes

like a vacant thought
i always had yet not nascent
enough to be recalled—

great waters have run
through me since
eons ago

before i was
while i am
where i stand

until one day
this river will flow
on its own —alone

III.

Of Paths Taken, Trails,
Traces, and Voyages

The Audrain Prairie

       Corn stubble, waiting winter wheat,
north of Auxvasse Creek, south of Salt River,
telephone poles, barbed and woven wire fences,
ornamental trees around houses, while grey scrub
oak, willow, elm, sumac persist along
channelized creeks at the edge of fields
where water runs only when it rains–
the feeder springs were sucked dry
a century ago, by deep water wells pumping
up the life source for irrigation, watering
crops, hogs, steers, and lawns.

       If I've crossed these sixty miles
of murdered prairie once, it seems a countless
hundred tedious times...

       Heading home in the waning light
of late December beneath darkening azure skies
crossed with white jet streaks, cirrus striations
fading into darkening violet tableaus, Orion
struggles to rise only a few million light years
above snow-dusted desiccated brown fields, when
a whirling murmuration of dark starlings dance
on wing between there and here over a soft pink horizon
in concerted chorographic motion between reflections
of earth and the deepening purple heavens—

       and I ask why until now have you
never shown me this beautiful wonder?

To Live and Die in New Mexico

Like blood running
from the heart
of the Sangre de Cristos,
the last of the red sun
slips away beyond
the dark Tres Hermanas.
Glowing orange embers dying,
dwindling, soft amber light wanes
as the earth fades
off to sleep into the deep
purple of a clear star-clad sky.

It is quiet now
across the Chihuahuan Desert,
only the crackling of a piñion fire
and arias of the coyotes to be heard.
El Sol is ever slow to resign his fate,
but rejoice; tomorrow morning
behold his resurrection.

Magellan

"On the edge of oblivion, all the world is Babylon,
all the love and everyone, a ship of fools, sailing on..."
                                        -Wang Chung,

all voyages, great and small, are fated—

youth is but a distant land
once one's crossed the 60th meridian.
No return after passage
through the Straits of All Saints,
at the end of your October, onward
into November, darkening December,
inflowing unfathomable waters
of relentless winter, navigating
immeasurable miles departed
memories, the years adrift,
all spent, how few farther
stormy leagues still ahead?
Yet, one last ocean to cross,
to that certain place on a critical coast
lies final fated Mactan where Lapulapu
awaits with poison dart and spear,
for you, suddenly near, now it is here,
and so far from the promises
of that distant embarkation
of exultations, of hope
and home, so far far away.

Sail on,
headlong toward
that setting sun, you sybaritic soldiers
of fortune, explorers of youth, naivety;
live, love, learn.
boldly, brashly, bravely,
blindly—
Sail on
before the abyss.

blue

> *"Compass, quadrant and sextant contrive*
> *No farther tides ... High in the azure steeps*
> *Monody shall not wake the mariner.*
> *This fabulous shadow only the sea keeps."*
>
> -Hart Crane, At Melville's Tomb

Beyond the ship's lacquered wooden rail
lie the remnants of a melancholic afternoon of
blue—

Filtered sunlight falls through watery
clouds of silver mists beneath
a glaucous gray sky, spreading above
dark navy waters, the same color as shale
in creek beds back home when the rocks
are dampened by seeping springs
through limestone seams.

Off the starboard aft mountains loom
over Olympic Peninsula like purple bruises
growing lighter in the distance before vanishing
into the subtle hues of a layered naval blanket
miasma of fog, mist, and rain vapors in various
denim shades so soft, imperceptibly growing murkier
as the soft evening shade falls.

The massive Pacific tide rises unstoppable
while barely noticeable from onboard a liner
in the Juan de Fuca, sliding in on swells

of nearly two feet ascending
with white flecked waves softly peaking,
when the brightest of chromatic golden light
floods across the ocean as the sun sets through
a sliver between the steel sea and the iron cloud sky
illuminating the briefest of harlequin moments:

black, white,
an orca and her calf rise,
spray they forcefully exhale
from blow holes shine
like glowing fountains
of light for only an instance
to complete that one instant
of a forever vision.

The whales rise once more
from the gloaming
only to lunge flukes up
and disappear, gone
as the sun declines,
skies fading to violet,
with midnight at its heels,
spreading shale grey shadows,
leaving nothing to be seen
beyond the floodlights
of the ship, to hear only
the rush of the wind, crash
of the water, the sirens'
singing their song of despair

and beauty that Odysseus
loved while lashed to the mast,
or was it the vision of the killer whales
rising from the darkness into the light
that called Hart home into the sea?
as they now call me,
from just beyond the rail,
out there in the dark rolling
midnight blue.

Greenland

Rocks; cold, black, grey, dark, unyielding
stone born two thousand million years
before Yahweh or Odin ever spoke.
Bits of ice and snow in striated shaded clefts
at the end of summer across a raw land
of fierce splendor. A glacial-cut channel,
jagged— sharp whetted winds whistling
through frigid fjords. The ship drifts silently,
frighteningly close between jagged icebergs
and metamorphic chisels in the narrows—
only metres from disaster
—of Prince Christian Sound,
named for a dead Danish royal.

Cathedrals of gneiss and granite cenotaphs
to ancient Stone Gods of the North who have
dwelt here for eons before men ever trod
this ice bound desolation, those emigrated immortals
still dwell within this frozen realm, alongside
the Norns, the Jörmungandr, the Giants of Frost
and Fire.

Yet the greatest, the native son who has lived here
since time immemorial, the true Lord of Arctic
     Dominion—
Nanuq, *The Great White Bear Who Wanders*
the cliffs, ice fields, shores, he blesses those children
who respect his domain, while hunting for lost fools

across his lands, those bewildered or left behind,
and they of dishonor whose time comes to leave
this cold world where monuments
to Our Great Bear God stand alongside
the legends of the Norse looming over dark waters
rippling beneath a dim arctic sun that bleeds
thru a ceiling of opaque clouds hanging
like grim boulders above incantations
from Inuit shamans and old Norse soothsayers
whose echoes call to me from far beyond
the dark ages—

      (i've been here in dreams
      since before i was a child so small
      genetic memory from beyond
      passed down from boreal lands
      on voyages across storm tossed seas
      hauling on frozen ropes beneath
      tattered canvas sails to landfall on
      dark isles of rocks beneath far-flung
      skies heavy upon my back pushing
      down into the ground i can't catch
      the wind i'm trapped struggling
      across jagged dark gravel shredding
      my hands knees chin scraping
      the rocks while crawling away
      to somewhere i don't know
      with a bleeding sky above me
      the Great White Bear follows
      my bloody trace of dishonorable

sin against this earth gaining upon me
in this serial nightmare years on and on
until one day catching me and if you die
in a dream you die in your bed but just when i am
certain all is over as the massive paw swipes
my head black claws rip my face open—
i am bolted awake, frightened, catching
my breath before a...)

— calm in the dark comes to my troubled
spirit on a mystical chant, a recalled mantra,
lifting me up out of the pain because only magic
could make anything survivable in this place where
i am but a tourist in truth or dreams, to be chewed up
by ruthless rocks, consumed by terrestrial elements
over long, horribly harsh hours; or perhaps death
comes in a few quick seconds, to end up
as polar bear dung washed away to the sea
with the slow snowmelt of spring.

rún

for Frankie Devine;
my brother in song and story.

There is no darkness as deep and long
as night at the end of December in Donegal
when the new moon sets in the gloom and gloaming

and the only light in the universe to fall
was born millions of years ago from billions
of stars and at night it sleeps in the snow

on the ridge of *Maol Mosóg* looming over
the pass of *Ghleann Gheis,* where the voices
of shadows whistle whispers on the wind

with songs and stories only elder druids and shamans
—the great grandfathers and greatmothers of we poets
and bards— can begin to translate from primordial
    tongues

in words older than the land, older than the bones
buried beneath the soil and stones in the backyard;
it would be of great hubris for false soothsayers
to speak of its knowledge

in such runic words— those mysteries of the ages,
the histories of human hearts born from dust of fallen
stars across a celestial plane until the foretold singularity

when all the light and dust will merge again—
    the prophecy;
will pass and reprise, pass and reprise, while
    the shadows
sing clear for the ages to hear primeval through
    the darkest of nights—

long beyond the short time we tread upon
    these rocks.

Éire go Brách

An ancient Irish philosopher
Kerryman, fisherman, cutter of sod.
a son of Brendan the Saint and sailor,
his eyes pale gray, white whiskers like wires
sprouting from the tip of his ruddy wind burnt nose,
imparted to me his take on it all—
history, legend, and lore in his quick,
clipped accent from the Dingle *Gaeltacht*
—over a pint and a pour
while we sat in a venerable pub by the sea
on a soft winter's day, late January,
Ballyferriter, County of Kerry,
together we watched
an early afternoon's red sun slide
through a slit in the sky
that parted between the wine dark ocean
and cold steel forged clouds
just beyond the Blaskets
at the end of the world;

> *If wishes were boats, once was a time*
> *we'd've all sailed away-*
> *from the blight upon this land*
> *with uncaring lords in London*
> *and Dublin who turned their blind eyes*
> *away be damned whilst*
> *a million died*

a million cried
a million went to Americay— '
His heavy finger, that of a man
who had heaved and hauled on nets
and ropes for more than half a century,
rapped the aged oaken counter
with every million lives he counted away,
eyes were watering a bit, like grey ice melting
with an ache as hard as turning a spade
to find spuds rotting in tainted soil
of *Black '47*, and with a daub
of a kerchief he wiped away
centuries of angst and loss
before turning to look back
into my sadly curious visage—

    'Ah, well you might know,
    when one leaves a place
    it kills a bit of those left behind;
    only the birds fly away
    and life stays the same—

Catching my breath in the back of the throat,
it fell upon me as I took a long drink,
swallowed hard the truth, one country's
boon was another's wound, while watching
the waning long rays of winter's sun
meet the sea—

Survival often requires
the breaking of hearts.

Up on the Inishowen

Ptolemy knew of this cold grey place;
Boreion on his map, the end of the north,
last of the knowable world, the wilderness
where edged rocks like teeth gnashed
the Atlantic into bits of splash and spray.

Stouthearted monks departed this headland
where grasses grasp for life, rowing out in skin boats
taking their faith northward to icy-watered know-not-
    where,
past the Hebrides, the Orkneys, the stormy Shetlands,
armed only with Brendan's sanction, guided by stars
to the Stones of Faroe, on to Iceland,
or further ashore on other lands
only God had known were yonder.

Imagine their joy at the sight of land! After many
    stormy weeks
tossed about like a leaf in the wind, with brothers lost
    at sea,

having to drink sheep's blood once freshwater was gone,
eating strips of mutton dried in the saltwater sun,
all of their corporeal sacrifices to get here and
    then—
their great grievous disillusion
—God had delivered them unto shores,
where they would die, without a soul to be saved,
but their own.

Staring out across that dark iron grey sea,
beneath churning, wind ripped skies, I wondered
what I would have believed if this, the end
of my only world? Would faith deliver me
unto lands of demonic monsters and devils,
into the hands of unlearned heathens that might
    lurk
beyond these tides —or only in my mind—
where Christ would have sent me unto them
forth to slay or save?

To Pour a Perfect Pint

"If yer in such a rush, have a feckin' whiskey."
—Padraig Eamonn Malone,
Publican/Founder, Paddy Malone's Pub

A perfect pint of stout takes time, patience, and a clean
   glass.

Stage 1: Hold the vessel at forty-five degrees
beneath the spigot, gently pull the handle
forward open allowing the full flow
to fill the jar four-fifths of the way,
no farther. Carefully release
the handle to stop the pour
just below the top
of the iconic harp.

   The flourish of infused liquid should be allowed
   to settle— the dancing surging nitrogen molecules
   must rest, the agitated beer must turn from cloudy
   and tan to clear and dark.

Stage 2 is poured slower:
Push on the handle rather than pull
allowing a slow silky stream of porter
to fall gently into the center of the creamy cap,
smoothly raising the head up to the top of the jar
with the subtlest of rounded crown just above the rim
without dribbling any of the brew over the edge.

Stage 3: A final rest is necessary to allow the last
bit of flourish from the latter pour
to settle, revealing a dark,
very deep ruby red
(if you do not look closely
you'll believe it to be black)
elixir beneath that creamy white head
of no more than five-eighths of an inch thick.

>Your first drink should be
>a deep quenching quaff—
>a restrained sip off of the head
>will not slake your thirst
>nor give the craft
>of your perfectly poured pint
>the veracity it deserves.

To pour a perfect pint
takes proficiency and patience,
two things the vast majority of Americans
seem to lack –oh, But not the Irish,
that steadfast, long-suffering lot
have learned to wait.

'When God made time, He made plenty,'
as cousins from the Copper Coast of Waterford
     remark,
and those from the gnarled fingers of West Cork's
Beara and Bantry grasping the Atlantic, are known
     to say,
'Relax, way dontcha? Wha' ha'e ye but to enjoy t'day?'

(...and then there are ancient Hibernians
known to lament of eight hundred years,
as they huddle in pubs from Dublin to Galway,
Killarney to Belfast, Kilkenny up to Derry,
from the tip of Dingle to the north
of Donegal true, with ex-pats
and descendants singing drunken lullabies
in Boston, New York, Chicago, too,
passing it on from the burning hearts
of shame-bearing souls with
blood-stained hands...)

After all these generations,
from Wolfetone to Emmett,
to Padraig Pearce and 1916,
from Mick Collins, up to Ger Adams,
and back to Boru—
What's da matter wit' ye not wantin' to wait?
Jes' two fuckin' minutes more for a
properly poured
pint?

Guiding Lights

Midnight in October I am drawn to these lights
like old friends from afar—
a string of stars
along the northwest horizon, beacons
from light years away, an amplified vista
just above the dark Boone County hills, viewed
through Earth's bended atmospheric lens.
Our galactic vessel sails through these galaxies
swirling at a million miles an hour
across an interstellar expanse
that knows no bounds.
The thought makes all the rest
seem small, petty; these pebbles
my bare feet must tread are suddenly
not so hurtful.

Men have followed these stars for a hundred
thousand years and more; migrating, hunting,
gathering, planting and harvesting by mystical lights
    above.
It is old Bootes I see, the Herdsman slipping away,
his brace of dogs nearly upon the Big Bear's tail,
lumbering north toward Polaris, where
the greatest of bears are known to live and run.
These old fables we once told ourselves
when gazing at moving lights in the night's sky
in the absence of knowing— we set them up

for a child's imagination to understand,
recited at bedtime, campfire stories,
the tales told and mythic machinations made
by mammoth hunters, Bronze Age sheepherders,
Greek oracles, Norse soothsayers, Celtic druids—
explanations for gaps in knowing what is truth,
what isn't dogma, orders to rule over the tribe,
clan, the plebes, call them what you will,
decrees thought and obeyed
with blind ignorance and the proud certainty
of faith that comes from the fear
of being a captive to unfettered control.

Whether it be a diviner who is to profess
from signs, planets, moons and stars
one is born beneath, or commands
from ancient scrolls by Pontifex,
or prayers demanded by priests reading
scripture from a book—
remember, it all began as a story,
a long time ago when someone
gazed up into the night skies
upon heavenly bodies
far, far away

The Towboat

              I pondered from our
bluff top upon a towboat,
cast to work below;

her knees pressed firmly to the bulkhead of a barge
as it's filled with sand dredged up from the river—
     sand
that had once lived in the snow melt of the Rockies,
or had settled upon the Great Plains to be blown
down across the Dakotas and Nebraska, or forced
by a deluge from a thunderhead over Iowa
or Kansas to runoff to the Waters of the People
of Wooden Canoes, the grains tumbling in fluvial
cacophony of Spring's symphony of high waters
until low water, slack water, they settle in the channel,
and Capital Sand Company sucks them up, deposits
them in tall conical piles upon the left bank of the
     river
where they stand like the pyramids along the Nile,
     until
deposited into the rust-colored barges,
to be pushed by the towboat thru the silt laden
current of this Missouri River, the screws churned
water so it spumed a creamed mud foam in its wake
as the small towboat worked the barge thru a flow just
two fathoms deep to a quarter league downstream
where swarthy deckhands in jeans and grimy t-shirts

waited under ill-fitting life vests, cables and
ratchets in their hands to build a tow of fifteen
barges laden with sand for a greater towboat
of the line to push downstream to someplace,
      somewhere,
wherever people don't have ample amounts of
sand in their lives.

        For a few moments,
watching their work– labors of men,
a pilot's deft skills–

softly I floated, letting the towboat carry
me downriver, almost a half century;
        I inhaled
the stagnant gasses released from the mud and muck
pulled up in the shallows by spinning blades, the screws
scraping the river bottom–
        I heard
the rumble and roar of twin diesels' boom, belching
up black befouling petrol fumes hanging upon
the wind like invisible gelatinous sheets
that you'd walk right through–
I felt
it on my skin, a slick membrane of fossil fuel,
to wear alongside the acrid odor of men
who'd heavily sweat and spit and swear and didn't
give a good goddamn if they'd stink, with bruised and
      scraped
shoulders from hauling lines, cables, gear with strong hands

and busted knuckles, mashed thumbs, the slip of
    a ratchet,
cables and lines break! Flies at supersonic speed,
steel and nylon whips, rips yer head off!
       Only stories perhaps,
yet completely plausible; one more thing lurching
in the back of a disquieted mind, blistering
in the sun, slogging through rain, running against
the wind; don't trip, fall, over the gunwale, over
the edge into that mire of doubt, alone with thoughts
on mornings fogged in, no wind, moored in place,
only the low constant vibration of diesel
engines through your feet, into your legs, torso, down
your arms, up into your head behind your eyes—
just stop fucking thinking about it.
Then, with the snap
of the flag on the jackstaff in my ear,
the wind is up, the fog lifts, the tow heaves
alive with creaks and groans as it launches
off the bank, into the channel, returning
to our labors, with that constant whooshing
wind in my face, and I struggle to move
away from the cage around my mind, just to hear
something else— perhaps a few sounds from home
upon the breeze that were free of the tow,
away from the rumble, the churn, the swoosh–
     yet always inescapable
among the monotonous
hours, days, immeasurable weeks, six hours
off watch, then six hours back on, never enough sleep,

long nights alone or awake for thirty days,
until dropped off somewhere downstream,
places you always thought you wanted to see;
Cairo,
Baton Rouge,
Natchez, Vicksburg,
New Madrid, Arkansas City –
and it's always a long road to get back home.

     I then shook
myself, returning to present predicaments,
watching the little towboat grinding her way back
upstream for another barge, there'd be another
after that, so I turned away,

     walked down to the pub,
back to these days, our times, more
liefsome years with you.

Echoes

Before last orders are called, I hope
to return to scenes once haunted,
to learn of, to listen, perhaps recover—

echoes
of songs sung with comrades that timbre
in revered college houses and halls—

echoes
of horse hooves rattling over cobblestones
along a foggy riverfront wharf—

echoes
of staccato raindrops and lulling Irish ballads
from an ancient pub while slipping silently as
    a shadow
down dimly lit Belfast lanes—

echoes
of birdsongs and woodpeckers rapping through
    the hollows
as I trace tracks up trails in deep darkened
Ozark hills—

echoes
of a paddle dipping in still water while guiding
a canvas canoe quietly across a smooth as glass water
at dawn upon misty lakes off the Gunflint Trail—

or am I only vaguely recalled by colleagues
of yore in passing conversations between
subsequent sips of aged drops of malt
over slackened lips on late evenings
in venerable pubs where if you listen
intently you will hear—

echoes
of old ghosts like me—

echoing
softly off the walls
as it is then that we
are most easily awakened.

IV

Of Kith and Kin

If I Know a Song of Missoura

*"Now I see the secret of making the best person: it is to grow in
the open air and to eat and sleep with the earth."*

— Walt Whitman

If I know a song of Missoura, would she know
a song of me?
Carefree vernal barefoot days along the banks
of the Mississippi,
with rumbling towboats, waters dancing,
their vibrations around my calves, massive wakes
of warm dark waves washing upon my thighs,
sand squishing between my toes like sprites,
youthful, running free.

If I know a song of Missoura, would she know
a song of me?
The quiet breath of bird dogs,
with my brother on Jim Quinlan's farm, the sun
sets beyond her Salt River hills, the dirt road
by the timber where quail covey in thick brush
before a single or two flushes out into the light
of a fading November's day, resounding
shotgun's boom echoes off the far
off bluffs, the sharp pungent smell
of smokeless powder,
the sweet acrid swirl
of Copenhagen wallowing
between cheek and gum,
the crackle of spittle, viscous and brown,
on frosted leaves of grass.

If I know a song of Missoura, would she know
a song of me?
The babbling of aqua green spring fed
Ozark streams,
flyfishing for rainbows on the Eleven Point,
catching smallmouth on the Big Piney,
the woosh of the line slicing
the air near my ear, the streamer landing softly
in the calm eddy at the edge of the flow,
as Brooks deftly ferries the canoe across
the current, placing me where I need to be,
before the strike, the run, the fight,
the leap and splash and dive and haul;
the dance of admiration before
contemplative release.

If I know a song of Missoura, would she know
a song of me?
The silence of frozen mornings
in the hardwood covered hollows
of home, a steaming mug of coffee in hand,
a flintlock musket at the ready across my lap,
the aroma of woodsmoke from the house beyond
hanging heavy in the air, from my stand watching
squirrels harvesting acorns while waiting
for wary whitetails, listening for the crunch
of careful cloven black hooves on dried icy leaves,
hear the snort of a buck echoing through the hills
on the edge of winter, breaking the silence
of a Ralls County morning.

And If I know a song of Missoura, would she know
this dirge of me?
Quiet conversations those last years
fishing, my grandfather and father, warm calm
evenings and their few final casts, anchored
on the back of *Pater Mississippius,* the songs
of summer birds in the shade along the banks;
squalling jays, tweetering cardinals, lowing
of mourning doves, rattling woodpeckers against
dead trees as dusk falls, to hear the fated barred owl
call our names, before the wistful night song
of the whip-poor-will guides
all we lost travelers home.

The Immigrant

He was very old when I knew him,
and I am old now, these memories
are somewhat muddled—

Years had long passed since his voyage alone
across an ocean away from his home
and the train bound over half a continent
brought him into a strange country,
a new hermitage in the *Land of Liberty*,
forever leaving behind
that island of *Terrible Beauty*
to work in a grey dusty industrial plant
on the western bank of a great river,
having sailed away from stormy seas,
bound and gone from Belfast in 1916,
before dying just a bit more
than a half century later.

He never spoke of home,
or the *Troubles*, with anyone.
Letters received from Donegal,
even late in his short-lived retirement
years, read but once, were crumpled by
his cracked gnarled hands, before he opened
the wood stove door, then tossed
the wadded stationary
into the flames, the words

of carefully scripted ink
from *Éire* afar would almost
instantly incinerate, up the flue
as abandoned smoke, floating away,
silently into the Missouri sky,
a quarter of the way,
and a lifetime,
around the world.

Mowing the Grass at Sycamore
Hollow Cemetery

My brother navigates the Lawnboy
deftly between the granite and limestone
markers. The grass is tall and thick,
he is careful not to tear into some still
fresh mounds of sandy loam, chert rock,
and clay not yet settled into the land

still open doors for the ghosts of sleeping relatives
and ancestors who come out to walk the paths down
the hill, where they whisper along the banks of
Sycamore Hollow Creek, their names known well
from local lore, some almost mythical;
Clarke, Dryden, Grant, Lee, Malone,
MacAllen, Tatman, Ward.

I coax the old red Tecumseh around prickly pears
and sisal near the resting place of Private Jesse Ward,
died in Vietnam, shot by a sniper, and Asher
    MacAllen,
the son of a great uncle— neither man did I meet,
although I knew of Jess from local gatherings –
ice cream socials, pot-luck dinners – when I was
    a kid.
Concerning Ash, as he was called, his name said
with the reverence of a saint. He fought in the Great
    War,

enlisted in 1918, at eighteen as old as the new Century
    itself,
a year older than I am turning this day; it's my birthday,
 there will be some small celebration later at home.
        (Everyone too busy keeping a roof over
        our heads to be concerned with trivialities
        such as birthdays.)

Ash died just a year before I was even thought of;
he was fifty-nine. They say it was from a war wound;
gas to his lungs in France. "Tough sonovabitch.
Took forty years to kill 'im." He survived with the scars,
labored with them, in the dust of that cement plant that
loomed over all our lives. He inhaled the miniscule
    elements of
lime and silica, cutting his tattered, battered bronchial
    tubes
and passages, advancing his destruction
over the last two score years of short-breathed life.
Not like Jesse Ward; when Jess died it was like a light
    switch
being snapped off. A bullet in the eye they said, no
    suffering.
How would they know that? He was also eighteen,
    drafted a Marine.
Both American heroes. Now they have their rest
just feet from each other beneath the cold rock and clay,
the broken remnants of two conflicts a half century
    apart
on the other side of the known world; they

answered the call
to stop the *Hun* and *Communism*. Ash put on his
    doughboy uniform
for every Fourth of July, Veterans' Day, and
    Memorial Day parade
to march down Broadway, even his last few, after
    he no longer
had the wind to walk, he rode in the Jeep.
Jesse never got a parade; he got a bullet to the eye
    and
a flag draped casket.
Both patriots answered the call.

After loading the mowers into the bed of the truck,
    I return
to Ash and Jesse with a broom, sweeping the minced
particles of grass away from their monuments,
    straightening
the small stars and stripes, "Old Glory," stuck in
    the ground,
left over from the Fourth of July almost two weeks
    past,
put there by the VFW. I stand, look, regard both
    graves
with veneration, and a restless crawling
questioning fear

We sit on the tailgate of the Chevy awhile,
in the shade of the cypress trees

looking at our melancholic finished chore,
chugging iced tea from a milk jug,
discussing maidrites at the Mark Twain Dinette
for lunch, as I stare up the drive at the headstones
wondering whose kids will mow the grass
after I am buried up along the ridge?

> "Do you think it wakes them?" my brother asks,
> "or disturbs them anyway? When we mow
> over their graves?"
> I shake my head,
> "Nah. After what all these people been through,
> I doubt they give a shit"
> "Gonna be the Army, Navy, or Airforce?"
> I froze. Spit Skoal juice on the ground. Shook my
>   head.
> "I dunno. They keep callin'. Even if it's
>   peacetime now,
> don't mean it will be tomorrow.
> Russians are liable to stir shit up
> in a jungle somewhere,
> if we don't first."

Morning is over, it's going to be a hot afternoon.
We have weeds to be pulled in the
garden. We agreed; Dad will be pissed,
but it is too hot to pull weeds today. And we'll get
an ass chewing, but we've learned to absorb
and deflect such.

Tonight, Mom will bake a chocolate sheet cake, fry
    up pork chops
and potatoes, served with fresh sliced tomatoes
    from the garden
with cottage cheese, and sweet corn roasting ears;
    my favorite dinner,
with the cake and vanilla ice cream after. I'll open
    a present,
then Sean and I'll go to town, Clemens Field,
watch the men's fast-pitch softball games,
maybe I'll see that girl. We'll drive past this cemetery
and the cement plant, both going and coming,
just as we do every living day.
And it will be an lingering while
before I stop this wondering what the ghosts of
Jesse and Asher might talk of when
the nights becomes cool, tranquil, and silent
along the banks of Sycamore Hollow Creek.

The Ironworker

Danny Doyle, for thirty-nine years, walking
high steel, a cat on a six-inch beam, rigging,
connecting steel structures rising
over the towns and rivers
of the Midwest Tri-States, drank his lunch
every day; icy cold six-pack, Budweiser cans
in his truck, with a shot of schnapps,
perhaps two, for dessert.
Calms my nerves, he'd say.

Cold afternoon in March, a week before
retirement, a gust of wind whooshed
through the steel skeletal structure,
Dan was mid-beam
his balance
faltered
he knew his fate—
falling silently
nine stories
       to the concrete pad below
          his head smashed first
          popped open splattering
          like a spilled strawberry malt
          before the blood oozed out in a dark
            pool
          as the others hopelessly descended
          to look upon their brother; they laid

a tarp like a canvas shroud, over a
  lifeless
Carhartt encased sack of bone,
blood, guts, flesh, piss, and shit.

The site superintendent called the police—
and O'Connell's Funeral Home.

My grandfather, Danny's life-long friend—
union brother-in-arms
—cleared the beer cans and liquor bottles
from the cab of his truck
before the police, coroner,
and hearse arrived
upon the scene.

Reliance

My mother canned tomatoes and carp in Ball Mason
    jars.
She'd make us soup and fry fish cakes on the worst days
of midwinter when frozen winds flew through shocking
    blue
skies and cheeks would be frostbitten— quick, burn,
    hurt,
even on short runs to the rick to get armloads of
    hickory, oak,
and ash for the stove to ward off the hoar frosts. The
    gusts
came roaring down the river, the wind chill hit like
    subzero rock,
freezing the horses' trough solid as the red mercury in
    the rusted
thermometer on the shed's wall dropped down to the
    bottom
of the bulb with a line so short you couldn't tell it was
    there.

My dad loaded his own shotgun shells and rifle rounds,
restocking stores of ammunition for next autumn's
hunting or the foretold impending end of the world.
There were thousands of fascinating casings
and cylinders, lead projectiles, bags of bird shot
alongside double aught, with cans of Dupont
    gunpowder

of varying grades strewn across his basement work
    bench.
My job was to hand him various items,
get his coffee, put sticks in the stove,
stay out of his way.
Trammel nets hung from floor joists to cement floors
like drab corded curtains the length of the basement.
I marveled at his heavily calloused hands deftly darning
the lines and as my soft fingers rubbed neatsfoot
    oil into
the resting horse tack waiting for spring. He'd listen
to country music of the fifties and sixties
through a beat-up Philco radio while he dipped
Skoal spiked with rum, and spit into a steel bucket
half-filled with sawdust. His scent of wintergreen,
Bacardi, Vitalis, sawdust and Right Guard still lingers
in my olfactory memory forty years on.
There were shelves and shelves that he had built
holding what seemed an infinite number of jars
of home-canned vegetables, fruits, jams, preserves,
and carp. Better fish— flathead, channel and blue cats,
walleye, crappie; from Salt River and the Mississippi
all hauled in over the gunwales the summer and fall
    before—
were kept with the beef, poultry, pork, rabbit, squirrel,
venison, upland birds and waterfowl— raised or
    hunted,
butchered and dressed, by our hands,
stored in twin freezer chests of steel
and white enamel.

A fire was kept going in the basement all winter,
keeping the floors above warm and propane bills
in check. Dad wouldn't let the dogs in the house,
but for those coldest of nights, he'd call for them
to go to the basement to sleep on old horse blankets
next to the stove, they'd curl up into tight balls,
their backs to the radiating dry heat. I would lay with
them— Jack the black and tan coonhound, King the
    massive
white German shepherd, and the English setters:
    Rambler
and Ranger. Although forbidden, I would sneak over
    and tune
the radio dial to KMOX AM and listen to Dan Kelly's
    clear
voice crackle over the airwaves, calling the St. Louis
    Blues
games from exotic places like Montreal, Toronto,
    Detroit—
his descriptions of power plays and penalty killing
    sizzled
through those cold nights, coming down to me in the
    dim
yellow-orange light from the fire glowing through the
    mica window
of the Ashley stove. I would fall asleep… holding the
    dogs, their breathing
and heartbeats in my ears below the radio's din… until
    my mother called
me upstairs. I'd hug and pet the dogs goodnight, quickly

turn the radio back
to WGEM, run up to the bathroom, shed myself
    of dirty clothes,
wash up for bed. I did as I was told.
    *

Snow falls soft on Antioch Hill where my parents
rest. They care no longer if the fires are lit, or
    mason jars
are stocked on shelves, or if their son writes verse
    as an artful liar.
The trammel nets of youth are wadded up in
    galvanized wash tubs
stored in the rafters of the new metal shed the old
    man built in his last years
tread upon his land, cared for now by my brother.
His guns were mostly auctioned
off, with only a few favorites kept, mementos of
    days shared, brothers and father
in fields, together on those few forever recollections.

The short version of American History reads
that the hungriest kept going West; my people
    stopped
halfway across the continent, on the west bank of
    a great river
in the middle of a land rich in resources where
    there was still some
bit of homesteads to be had. The story of my kith
    and kin is brief
and terse: self-reliance.

We never had much money, but
no one would ever dare to say—
upon the pains of a fuckin' busted nose
or the curse of a river-bottom backwoods witch,
    or worse
— that we were poor.

Affirmation

I'm sorry he never showed you any
    affirmation.
          she said
over medium rare ribeyes and blood red wine
      at Mike Shannon's, before we went
      to the Cardinals-Mets game; she had yet
      to see the new ballpark, already six years old,
      having opened the spring before Dad died.
Considering her words,
      I took
      a good mouthful
      of dry zinfandel and held it
      with my thoughts
      for just a beat
      then swallowed hard
          the forever unspoken truth
      hidden just behind my eyes,
      always seen when I gazed hard
      into the fractured glass of the mirror
      I had walked upon His entire life,
          wondering?
          Who was staring back at me?

With pulse settled, hairs relaxed
      on back of my neck, I sat
      the goblet down, sighed and
      I smiled –

for her.
It was a long time ago,
she was just a kid. No need for
guilt now; she wasn't well, we would
say goodbye too soon enough—
still—

   He showed it in his own way…
I assured her.

   He was a good dad.
   There was always
   food on the table,
   clothes on our backs,
   shoes our feet.
   He bought me that the pair of elk-hide
   Nocona's when I finished college.
   He let me use the Remington 1100
   for goose and duck hunting.
   He loved that shotgun.
   So did I.
   He took me out on the river,
   fishing… if I'd ask… and
   He bought me two puppies—

an English Setter and a Blue Tick hound;
  both were hit by cars.
  for a month of Sundays I always
  went to bed crying myself to sleep
  believing it was my fault they died;
  I hadn't kept an eye on them,

hadn't taught them to look out for cars
when crossing the road.
There was never a strong hand
of comfort on my shoulder
to settle a not-yet-tempered heart.
No one ever said it was because
those drivers were going too fast
on the blacktop through the village
they weren't paying attention.
No one ever said sometimes
dogs chase cats and squirrels
in front of cars.
No one ever told me
that I wasn't a complete fuck up
that it was okay to be sad
or different or daydream
No one ever
affirmed
that I was not the mistake that
I believed.

Salvation

for Deirdre.

It must be in the blood. Shirley
stood at the alter three times:
Catholic, Baptist, and Vegas. Finally
she learned how to argue
over mashed potatoes without
consulting an attorney. Sterling
built up a farm from mud
along Salt River, raised three sons
before the flood and foreclosure.
He lost everything
keeping a second wife
and paying alimony. Dorie
lost Uncle Richard when the Buick flew
off the road, leaving her and D.K.
to make it alone. Grandma
would cuss on Saturday night
while Grandpa dressed up
for the Star Club: his red bow tie
and grey fedora. His heart gave out
while waltzing in the arms
of a sleek-legged girl. Mother's
annulment was secret till
I read the tattered clipping hidden
in her senior annual. My brother
filed at the courthouse three months
after we tied empty beer cans
to his truck.

D.K. is thirty-two, still alone
with little need for men. I lie
at night sweating, rolling among
wadded sheets, my eyes searching
the dusty tiles for a face, a home
with two-point-five children,
get-away weekends at the lake,
a fireplace to sit before
and hold hands,
till death do
us part.

The Ralls County Line

Born a restless spirit beside a river running far and wide,
a curious mind of *'where's and why's,'* wandering
toes ready to roam from the town of Huck and Tom
who stood on the end of Main Street in bronze
strolling onward, bolstered by Buster's tales
of adventures faraway, jumping the railcars
during The Depression's darkest of days,
stories calling onward, as if to Odysseus,
fated to Gods of fortune and failure,
riches and ruin.

At eighteen, you pulled on traveling boots,
yearning to thrive, leaving family, friends,
old truths, old lies behind, in a cloud of gravel dust
into the sky, with tire smoke, out of sight, *(but always*
in the back of your mind.) With an old duffel bag
packed, a full tank of gas in a blue GMC
four-wheel drive, burning up blacktop,
leaving loves and lives, as you'd drive away,
crossing the Ralls County Line.

Over highways, back roads, turnpikes, trails,
and traces away— down to the Delta of Mississippi
you rode on the back of the Father of Waters,
and up *La Belle Rivière* – the Ohio Beautiful—
as a river horse saddle tramp through younger days
of some quixotic design. They let you go in St. Louis

you headed west over Oklahoma on to Texas
high plains far and wide, up to Thunder Basin
and the Bighorns of Wyoming, through South Pass
crossing the Great Divide. Wanderlust—
the ethos of the era— burning daylight,
midnight oil, gasoline, a hole in your pocket,
never enough money, but you could always
make more,
and never a thought
that you'd run out of time,
because death is just a distant rumor
to the younger mind.
With one day running into the next,
just wake up to another, but like sand slipping
through your fingers, the river will take it away
the tighter you grip the less that will stay, yet
you kept rambling down those roads, floating
on those streams, dreaming, drifting
like a thunder cloud across
north Missouri prairie skies,
farther and farther away
from the Ralls County Line.

But there comes a morning awakened,
thirty years gone by, throw your head back,
howl, cry, and wonder *why?you spent your life
    asleep?*
tossed it away? It took too long to finally find a
    mate;
she's held you close, now, between the rattle,

rush, ruin,
rubble, silence,
and screams,
those days with thoughts of halfway walks
across the bridge, don't take the dogs
because you're not coming home.
You could always foresee
happier days, settled, you'd make it all right,
you'd make it good. *But what does that mean?*
     You buried
all those hours, years you could keep locked up, saved
for some distant rainy day. But it doesn't work that way.
You danced, played, drank the time away.
Why couldn't it all stay?
Why are the rest all gone and you
are still here to stray?
Why do years grow shorter as you leave
them behind? Why were you not taught the fragility
of time when you still had plenty of a young life to live
back home across the Ralls County Line.

There comes a dawn on a wistful whippoorwill's call,
just above the memory of a fiddle's lament
with oak and hickory campfire memories
like wafting smoke in soft purple light,
with the haze of the whiskey
and the warm buzz of the weed,
and you're awake to the state of being;
just move ahead from here—
there's days of wine to be drunk

fish to be caught, a world yet to live
and there's still time, and there's that yearning
to be back there, where we all belong, at least
in your mind,
across the Ralls County Line.

More years gone now than lie ahead,
hard truth the mirror does not belie, the lines
on your face, compadre gray hair— always waxing
towards white —will not deny; the road is short that
    lies ahead,
with battered knees, knuckles, the breaks that healed
    bad,
they do not lie. Where has it all gone? nearly half
    a century
since you lit out for those far-flung fates
out there, far away, leaving kith and kin
and clan behind, and now this journey
dwindles to the end, the last chapters
written with a shaky hand,
these half-remembered
stories, dreams… left in the dark corners
of your mind, and the road leads back,
toward, and over,
the Ralls County Line.

One morning the sun will dawn over that big river
of your youth, and that bell will toll to which you
will not arise. But Spring will return with blossoms
and foals, Summer will flourish with weeds and vines,

until Autumn comes to harvest what was once green
and alive. The leaves will tumble, fall softly, on the
    breeze
through the branches of cottonwoods and sycamores
in the slough bottom beyond childhood's backdoor,
short days in December settle in and the good
Winter's rest finally calls, pastures sleep fallow,
rivers flow low to the sea, all things merge,
the land, the water, the sky, and the stars,
are destined to finally entwine and the boys
pack you up to carry you down over the bank,
where they lay your ashes down
upon that warm dark green flow,
take you home, finally settled,
for all time, back across
the Ralls County Line.

Poem in an Envelope

My brother found the poem—
he brought it to me
before Christmas;
You died
just before Xmas—
twelve years ago.
You had kept the poem in an envelope,
so long, what once was white now
antiqued ivory, aged, brittle, dusty,
for forty years, stuffed in a larger manila
envelope along with a birth certificate,
high school diploma and school vaccination
records; childish mementos, worthless today,
archival antiquities, you stashed,
hidden away— of me.

hidden

You must have found my forgotten poem—
i certainly don't recall giving it over to you
—Perhaps it was in the drawer
of my corner desk of affordable laminate wood
once gifted with hopes that i might sit at it
to become a writer of renown or scholar,
neither occurring in any discernible estimation.

discernible

Upon examination, i am certain that it wasn't
presented to you; there were traces
of white-out and pencil erasures from notations
and mistakes (many made over all these days).
i wouldn't have left something so flawed
to posterity in the event of a fatal
car crash or accidental overdose.

accidental

It obviously meant something to you or why
keep it? i always seemed the family's accident,
the triangular peg in the square hole. But you
understood my desires, interests so different,
but couldn't really encourage me, or push me,
or help me towards the things
that the men in our world did not do
lest be singled out. i understood you not
knowing how – nor did i – to stand tall
against such a deep world of shallow vision,
going back to that day when i expressed
what -i wanted- yearned to be.

yearned

You took a breath, through
your teeth, poured us each
a whiskey and exhaled a sigh,
as you passed me the glass.

You took a long drink.

"Let's not tell your father,"
was all you knew to say.

Looking Over the Missouri at Dusk

It is strange and sad to still be alive,
the elder of a family line, but also
still a child, lost, alone, left behind,
just five years from the age which
the old man died, five years before
getting in and out of the boat
will become difficult, as well
as unwise.

Dad was a craftsman, a welder,
smoked Winston's before he grew ill,
yet spoke of the poisons of neither.
Stoic and strong, stability certain,
he provided all that was needed,
more than he as a child
had known, but—
He wielded shouts and silences
over me like sticks at a cornered
cowered dog; delivering
or withholding, they battered
a frail hearted boy all the same.

But at dusk, when the river flowed low
and the flatheads begin to bite— *wait,
set the hook*— together
we hauled in big ones up over the gunwale,
onto the deck of the jon boat, both of us happy,

smiling, still, forever in black and white memories,
dark as bats chasing elusive dust-winged moths
in and out of sight, but always there
forever faithful
upon the wall.

The air is cool now, my breathing clear,
and dewy fatigue sneaks in. A whistle
for the dogs and turn away
from the river's flow—
remorseless, ceaseless
—toward home, *home*, we go
where a good part of this life
might still be wrought.

V.
Of Lessons Learned,
Life, and Loss

a skiff of snow

a skiff of snow was blowing
over the blacktop
upon bitter gusts from across the plains;
pulled my collar against the chill,
turned the other cheek—
knew she wasn't coming home,
again, today.
the roaring of the whiskey still echoed
thru the hall; apologies lay fallow on the floor.
yesterday's coffee -like yesterday's words-
brewed bitter cold and strong; i stood
drinking the hard truth
staring out an open door.
starkness in the rooms mirrored that within
the heart, anger's plowed furrows of hate
bore indifference– a harvest of lies
brought forth steel disdain, cold
as the breath on the north wind—
it was time to pull the last string.
it fell apart in a moment yet lingered thru the night
before the shadows of a snowy dawn
where it just drifted away
into tumbling skies of a pallid grey
wash over fallow frigid fields.

> the dead elm
> at the end of the drive, stood sentinel
> to the end of our song.

Indian Autumn

The air is cool for August; Octavian's month
of self-aggrandizement. We still swelter
beneath his empirical name two thousand years
on, but don't be fooled.
Just as Sirius glimmers in a dog day's night,
the second Caesar's heat will return—
for now, enjoy the respite

of this tribute sent southward to us,
from the Assiniboine,
knights of the Northern Steppes,
and the Ojibwe warriors,
the trappers and trackers
of the Northwoods,
builders of birchbark canoes,
sending us cool winds coming down
off a boreal landscape since
the land awakened from receding
glaciers, leaving high wide and wild
great plains and prairies of bison
since dissected, ploughed over
and over into our dry dusty fields
of corn and grain growing gold
in late summer sun before harvest,
a bounty soon hauled by rail across
a continent or towed downstream
in barges on the back of the great river

we call *Missouria*— named for the
'People of the Wooden Boats'
—flows

beneath the bluff below
our backyard, where birddogs dance
flushing doves and songbirds away
from thriving vines of Virginia creeper
and morning glory alive in the mellowed
sun so fair, with crisp unfettered air,
breathed deeply into clear lungs, so rare
in the usually heavy atmosphere
and humidity always endemic
this time of year.

The fiery wrath of Caesar Augustus
will return, if not this week, next, but
be presently pleased in the calm
of his retreat, soon we will return
to living under his harsh rule.
Yet time is short until November,
Octavian's ninth month we count
as the eleventh, with its frost and chill,
when we will call with thanks
to the People of South Winds—
the Kansa, Kiowa, Comanche
—for warmth, like a Navajo blanket
and their always much-welcomed gift
of Indian Summer.

Summer Fades

As the days grow short in mid-September
the heart-shaped leaves of the morning glories
lose their love – weaken, wrinkle, wither;

the trumpeting blossoms don't resound lustrously
to meet the day, fading violet in falling dusk
turns to rusted grey— dying, dull, dusty

and I soon to be tearing the vestiges of skeletal vines
still clinging from the fence and walls at autumn's end,
leaving their smallest trace of tracks and designs

of memories and shades of memories to hide
behind the chilled skies of winter, mirages
to catalog alongside the reprise

of strewn scenes and seasons gone by,
all those scattered moments left to
recollect beneath the once radiant arbor.

Prehistoric

My bones have not yet petrified—
No paleontologist has yet catalogued
this life. Of the few who have looked
over the body, none seem to understand
its existence. Admittedly, a strange
creature it must seem, being
of the past, yet not far enough back
to pique morbid curiosities. The record
of years spent over different disparate
lives, loves, longings, ending
in a boneyard, shards of memories
scattered, spread across deserts
of time, runes scratched
into horn and bark, scrawled
onto hides and clay.

No one created this, only evolution,
a product of settings over time,
collection of remains, more dug up
each day, as the pen scratches
the page.

Perhaps some see
it too simple, dim, antiquated,
this nature of being, a missing
link between here and some
where out there, not worth

consideration by august scholars
out digging in these fields,
learned are they and bright
as billions of stars flying
high in night skies.

They look down from above
upon the dirt where I dwell.

History

Taught always in elementary days
"To (you MUST) Believe" these men
to be Gods of noble ways— Giants
of the eternities, who tread across centuries,
with rapt intent by sanctified epistles of veracity
and boundless treaties of infamy, levied and led
trusting armies through fields, forests, plains, and prairies
to sacrifice the youthful of patriotic society to be bled
upon a hubristic alter of *Manifested Destiny,*
the flesh of nations and lands slaughtered
with most awe full machinations while generation
after generation of dark women and men,
as dark as life-giving earth, clamped into chains
that smelled of rusted iron mixed with the bitter blood
of their being, their spirits shackled from fleeing,
forced into labor and labored in fettered fields
of hopeless hours and darkened days—
soon joined by the tired huddled yearning to be
exploited burned alive in the all-consuming avarice
of capitalism, locked inside a garment sweat shop fire
or blown to bits in darkest tunnels mined through
    mountains
deep and wide as they drudged with toils to carve
    with pride
the immortal visage of the conquerors of a continent
across the face of *Pahá Sápa*— those dark captured
    sacred hills

stolen from the seven bands of the Lakȟóta —
    with magnificent
roads laid down over once sacrosanct trails now
    leading
to a park where we gaze upon remarkably awe-
    some (awe-ful)
busts standing tall as towers as we read the plaques
    and gaze
at paintings, their trophies of times and place so
    we always
must remember their greatness and glory, these
    never-ending
gifts of guilt given over and the dire duty of
    knowing
that upon this heap the bed is made
where I must sleep.

My Crooked Face

My crooked face slides slowly from my skull,
its blemishes like barnacles attached
to a hull, and the clouts to my nose
from those many years ago have grown
pronounced in gravity's throes.

Fat and feeble, my feet have foundered;
if i were an old horse at this late hour
i'd be led behind the shed, given a pat
on the withers before being
shot in the head.

Dark auburn hair has faded to a whiter shade
of pale, while once boyish, roguish good looks
used selfishly in betrayal - what can i say?
now all those trite tropes washed away,
since you gave away a hopeful heart,
since you let me know you,
since our first embrace.
Off to hell then with all intentions, good
or bad, that paved that goddamned highway
we once tread; believe me when i say
it was true. i was never that clever,
never would or could have been, given
my demons, desires, dysfunctions—
cursed, hurt, broken, with a void i
didn't know how to fill, i

didn't know how to love. i
was hurtful to us both but
more so to you. i

am sorry i never could say goodbye,
suppose my hell awaits in this way
or the other, but i have always held out
for hope that your memory of me
was to be always as beautiful
as mine is of you.

Rainy Night

The blacktop shimmers
beneath the wash of the security lamp
at the T intersection of routes N and E.

Back in the shadows, the old schoolhouse looms,
once whitewashed, now peeling, drowning
under a leaking roof, abandoned in the gloom.

Just a ghost from another century, as apparitions
of parents and grandparents when children they were,
as we were children years gone by, all playing together

in a schoolyard of memories, ethereal pale outlines
darting in and out of the falling rain like vague eels
writhing, trammeled in a net, slapping their tails,

startled spectres' dead eyes staring up to nothing,
only the hiss of raindrops falling over the canopy
of cottonwoods, maples, and sycamores, spread

above the black current rushing
through the creek beneath the bridge,
in the damp darkness beyond sight—

waters rolling roaring rising
into already flooded bottoms
of late spring, so much noise

indistinct voices babbling
across the open yards, calling
us home

when I awakened in a sweat soaked shirt
in that old familiar void, before the dawn,
lightning flashes, thunder follows—

and I wish for nothing more
than hear your voice,
again, but that would be
a long-distance call
too far.

Unrequited

and yet, yes
i think of you often.
it starts. hesitates. stops
in measured doubt
as the sun sets to meet
those far off hills looming
a lifetime away.
as i shudder to think
on the vacuous tomorrows
spent wandering
aimlessly toward the cold
Missoura clay.

A Dream of Driftwood & Other Thoughts

On a sandbar i awakened
before dawn to hear a mountain lion's scream
from the bluffs above & beyond the deep woods
bringing a silence of fear to every living thing
along the river running dark to avoid possible
        discovery
by the apex predator like the fear of a haunting
        ghost
that can't be remembered when waking up but
it is always there until the chorus of crickets & frogs
returns to bathe & bury me in flood of sound
                as the quiet light
                    of dawn whispers pink & blue above the
                        trees
on the Illinois side the dim glow illuminates pieces
        of driftwood
dead bleached bare & white the skeletal remains
        of giant sycamores
& cottonwoods & maples— the great beings that
        once lived
along the banks of this omnipotent leviathan of
        a stream
but it pulled them into their graves while still
in the prime of their life only because
they had the audacity to live along the edge of it all
                when downstream
                    there's a cacophony & i turn to see a murder
                        of crows

cawing & diving at a lone owl in the top of a tall cypress
    tree
the corvids in beastly black descended like a mob of
    demons
tormenting a soul in some verdant hell until the wise
    child of Athena
takes leave of such temporal nuisances flying further
    into the woods
the crows chase for a few futile strikes but one by one
    fall away
disappearing into the thick timber as emergent daylight
    signals
a chorus of cardinals & redwing blackbirds & orioles &
    meadow larks
& scolding bluejays over & over each other as they raise
    their voices
from the backwater sloughs
        singing to their Great God
        of living & light who turns flowing water
from night's dark blood black to morning's olive-green
    brown
colors of earth & life with cream colored foam along *le
    Grand Fleuve's*
edge i'm strolling sipping imported instant americano
    from a tin cup
looking at fragile fish bones & striated mussel shells
    alongside small chips
of driftwood & nature's other jetsam & flotsam at the
    edge like
Shoeless Joe from Hannibal MO my barefoot steps
    leaving tracks

forever behind then i remember why?
we all must rise to our River God— Father
     Mississippi
               —all the rest is merely the décor surrounding this
               untamable behemoth who will eventually
                    awaken
               in the great flood to wash this world away.

Jude MacAllen Tatman is a Missouri poet, historian, and publican, born in Hannibal and raised on the family homestead along the west bank of the Mississippi River. He received his BA in History, with an English minor, from Northwest Missouri State University, and earned his MFA in Creative Writing with the University of Nebraska at Omaha's Writers Workshop.

Past vocations include work as a farmhand, union Ironworker's hand (Local 577, Burlington, Iowa), deckhand working on the barges of towboats on the Mississippi and Ohio rivers, pizza delivery driver while also playing a season and a half of semi-pro baseball in West Texas, waiter and bartender, corporate sales and marketing, and an archivist/historian for Missouri State Parks. He also lost on Jeopardy.

MacAllen and his wife, Marilee, own and operate Paddy Malone's Irish Pub in Jefferson City, where they live with a brace of bird dogs on a bluff overlooking the Missouri River in a century-old bungalow that belongs to a couple of somewhat ornery cats.

This project was made possible, in part, by generous support from the Osage Arts Community.

Osage Arts Community provides temporary time, space and support for the creation of new artistic works in a retreat format, serving creative people of all kinds — visual artists, composers, poets, fiction and nonfiction writers. Located on a 152-acre farm in an isolated rural mountainside setting in Central Missouri and bordered by ¾ of a mile of the Gasconade River, OAC provides residencies to those working alone, as well as welcoming collaborative teams, offering living space and workspace in a country environment to emerging and mid-career artists. For more information, visit us at www.osageac.org

www.ingramcontent.com/pod-product-compliance
Lightning Source LLC
Chambersburg PA
CBHW031136130726
47988CB00006B/2396